The Complete Ministry Audit

HOW TO MEASURE 20 PRINCIPLES
FOR GROWTH

William M. Easum

Bonus: Spreadsheet Disk Included

ABINGDON PRESS
NASHVILLE

THE COMPLETE MINISTRY AUDIT
HOW TO MEASURE 20 PRINCIPLES FOR GROWTH

Copyright © 1996 by Abingdon Press

This book is printed on recycled, acid-free paper.

ISBN 0-687-01817-X

00 01 02 03 04 05—10 9 8 7 6 5 4 3 2

MANUFACTURED IN THE UNITED STATES OF AMERICA

Contents

CONTENTS

Section Four: After the Study

Appendixes

The Top Ten Reasons for Using the Complete Ministry Audit

1. It works!

2. You have at your fingertips the knowledge that William Easum has gained from more than five hundred local church consultations.

3. Once you purchase this workbook, you have permission to copy all of the data-collection forms for distribution throughout your congregation (but no other congregation).

4. You have a diskette containing spreadsheet files to make data collection easier.

5. You can save thousands of dollars by not having William Easum or one of his team come to your church for an on-site consultation.

6. The Complete Ministry Audit provides you the tools you need in order to think and act strategically about your congregation and its mission.

7. The Complete Ministry Audit provides you a proven step-by-step process for developing disciples.

8. The laity are personally involved in the process of arriving at the recommendations.

9. You don't have to leave home.

10. Many church leaders say that it is the most comprehensive tool available.

Section One

GETTING STARTED

Thinking Strategically

Thinking and acting strategically today is not as easy as it once was. Change itself is changing so fast, and present-day culture is becoming so indifferent, even hostile, to Christianity, that effective church leaders can no longer rely on traditional ministries to grow disciples. If churches are to continue nurturing and discipling people, they will have to find new ways to reach believers and pre-Christian people with the old gospel.

The Complete Ministry Audit is designed to help you make assessments and improvements in your congregation's ministries. The twenty principles related to church growth described in section 2 are discussed in greater detail in my book *The Church Growth Handbook* (see Recommended Reading). The planning group that is leading the planning will benefit from at least one copy of the handbook, and key members of the group may need their own copies of *The Complete Ministry Audit*.

The process suggested is more a diagnosis than an evaluation. The team that is leading the planning will act more as a physician than as a counselor. Doctors diagnose and prescribe. They do not make value judgments. Sometimes the prescription is a remedy, and sometimes it is preventative medicine. But never is this kind of assessment a value judgment about the persons involved. The same is true about the Ministry Audit. The task is not to make a value judgment about the congregation, but to make a diagnosis. The process ends with strategic recommendations about what church leaders can do to improve or remedy their ministry.

This workbook, *The Complete Ministry Audit*, is the basic tool that you will use in arriving at a diagnosis and prescription. As you go through the book, remember to look for patterns that jump out at you, and do not get lost in too much detail.

I strongly recommend that you get a demographic profile of your area that includes information about the trends and lifestyles of the people who live within ten miles of your church. Percept offers one such profile (see Recommended Resources for information on ordering). It is extremely difficult to decide what new ministries to begin without information about the surrounding community. Very few longtime church members are in touch with the unchurched world around them. Effective churches do not ask the congregation what new ministries to begin. Instead, they discover felt needs in the community and develop quality ministries to respond to those needs.

Your initial preparation requires the following three steps:

____ 1. Select the Steering Team
____ 2. Survey Worshipers
____ 3. Survey Church Officers

First, Select the Steering Team

Select a steering team of seven people, including the pastor, to take responsibility for this process from start to finish. Your team will be responsible for the following:

1. *Collecting the data for the Ministry Audit, which includes responsibility for*
   a. the worship survey;
   b. the data contained in worksheet number 1;
   c. giving out and collecting the leadership surveys contained in worksheet number 2 and averaging the responses;
   d. transferring all of the above data to the Ministry Audit itself;
   e. analyzing the Ministry Audit and arriving at recommendations;
   f. sharing the information and recommendations with church leaders;
   g. encouraging the church leaders to take action on the recommendations.

2. *Securing outside resources* that might be necessary to answer any questions that arise or to provide options for any situation that might arise. A lengthy resource list is enclosed at the end of this document.

Order at least one copy of *The Church Growth Handbook* for the steering team. You can get this from your local Christian bookstore, or you can order it by calling 1-800-672-1789.

Second, Conduct the Worship Survey

Make enough copies of the Worship Survey, pages 64-65 (or print, from the software disk, the file named "WORSHIP.*"), to distribute to the anticipated number of worship attendees over four consecutive Sunday services. After all of the surveys have been completed, calculate the averages and turn to pages 101-128 of this workbook and record the information on the Ministry Audit.

If you use the spreadsheet file ("WRSHPENT.*"), simply enter the numbers into each cell, and the spreadsheet macros will do the calculations for you, so that a report can be printed and the numbers then inserted on the master audit.

Third, Collect Information from Church Leaders

Decide how you are going to gather the information that is asked for in the Ministry Audit worksheets from the official body—that is, the church board, the administrative board, the elders, the session, or however you designate the body of church officials.

1. Some collect the information at a meeting of the official body; others mail it to the members of the official body. You will get more returns if you have the members fill out the survey at a meeting.

2. You would be wise to recruit only one person to have responsibility for the statistical work. With access to a personal computer that runs Windows 3.1 or higher and uses Lotus or Excel (or with knowledge of how to port the files into another spreadsheet program), this person can make good use of the spreadsheets on the disk bound inside the back cover of this book.

The **Staff Worksheets** can be found on pages 66-89.

The corresponding spreadsheet files on the bonus disk are "STAFF1.*" (Staff Worksheet), "STAFF2.*" (Staff Readiness Worksheet), and "STAFF3.*" (Staff Permission Giving Worksheet).

> The **Official Body Worksheets** can be found on pages 90-100.
> The corresponding spreadsheet files on the bonus disk are "BODY1.*" (Official Body Worksheet), "BODY2.*" (Official Body Readiness Worksheet), and "BODY3.*" (Official Body Permission Giving Worksheet).

Give copies of the Official Body Worksheets to each member of your official body. There are three separate worksheets: (1) the Official Body Worksheet, (2) the Official Body Readiness Worksheet, and (3) the Official Body Permission Giving Worksheet.

Have someone collate the answers, preferably your statistician and someone else to help, and fill out one master copy that averages the answers. Because of the one to ten scaling factor on these worksheets, the answer will be a number derived by averaging the responses. Insert the averages into the proper places in the Ministry Audit, pages 101-128.

If you prefer to use the spreadsheet on the disk that is bound in this book, your spreadsheet program will use the macros (sums and averages) to average the responses for you. This data can then be associated with other surveys and printed for a report.

Give copies of the Staff Worksheets (pages 66-89) to each person who is a paid member of your staff. The collated answers to the questions on these worksheets will be recorded on the Ministry Audit, pages 101-128. Some of the questions require research into the membership records that your church keeps on worship attendance, stewardship, and other kinds of data. You may prefer to divide up this data research among members of the staff. These questions are focused on informational data, both historical and current. A spreadsheet file for collecting data is supplied for the Staff Readiness Worksheet ("STFF2ENT.*") and the Staff Permission Giving Worksheet ("STFF3ENT.*").

Once the questions for both the staff and the official administrative body are answered, they can be transferred to the Complete Ministry Audit, pages 101-128. The task will make more sense if the person compiling the Complete Ministry Audit has read section 2 of this book, and that material can be supplemented with a reading of *The Church Growth Handbook*.

Understanding the Complete Ministry Audit

Two Types of Questions

Type One Questions. The numbered questions marked by asterisks are *subjective questions* that have no right or wrong answers. These questions deal with perception and do not have measurably accurate or inaccurate responses. They are answered on a scale of 1 to 10, with 1 indicating total agreement with the question and 10 indicating total disagreement. Any response below 4 is a yes, and any response above 6 is a no. Any response from 4 to 6 shows a near split on the answer. A response of 5 often indicates that the respondent did not have a strong opinion about the question.

When the numbers are tabulated, wonder aloud if the overall scores suggest a pattern? Are the numbers consistently close to the same? The vast majority should be heavily weighted toward a yes answer. Look for those things that jump out at you and your team.

I have supplied the average scores for all these type one questions. These averages come from the scores of more than two hundred congregations throughout the United States. If your church is in Canada, add .30 to each of these averages.

Any score that is more than .50 above or below the average is outside of the norm for that answer, either positively or negatively. For example: If the average score is 3.56 and your score is 4.78, it is outside of the norm to the negative side and could indicate a weakness that you need to address. If the average is 3.05 and your score is 3.35, you are within the norm. If the average is 3.0 and your score is 2.2, you are outside of the norm to the positive side. That is excellent. How the scores compare to the scores of hundreds of other churches is what gives them positive or negative characteristics. If you are outside the norm to the negative, that does not mean that you are "bad." It simply means that you need to look more closely at the factors that pushed you outside the norm.

In most cases, it is wise to look at the overall patterns instead of at individual scores. However, some of the individual scores merit special attention. All of the crucial questions are explained in the study guide, section 2.

If you have many scores that range between 4.7 and 5.3, your church leaders may disagree about the issues raised, or be unsure about many of the answers.

Analyze the responses to these type one questions for patterns, and see where you stand on individual issues.

Type Two Questions. The numbered questions without asterisks tend to be more *objective*, that is measurable, than those with asterisks. The answers to these questions come from records within the church and from the survey taken in worship. These answers deal more with fact than with perception.

Throughout the Ministry Audit reference will be made to traditional and nontraditional churches. Traditional churches rely primarily on Sunday school, have worship primarily on Sunday, use traditional liturgical forms of worship, and do not stress small groups in homes and contemporary worship. Nontraditional churches stress small groups in homes, practice contemporary worship (synthesizers, no hymnals, drums, drama, interviews, and so on), and may or may not stress adult Sunday school.

Decide which type of church you are: (1) traditional, (2) nontraditional, (3) moving from traditional to nontraditional, or (4) moving from nontraditional to traditional. Many of the actions you will want to take in response to the Ministry Audit depend on which one of these categories you choose.

Twenty Growth Principles

The Ministry Audit is organized according to twenty growth principles. Not all of these are important to each church. It depends on your church's stage of development. You will know which ones apply to you when you finish filling in the Complete Ministry Audit.

Key Questions

As you analyze the audit, you will notice that within each growth principle are listed several key questions.

My experience has taught me that some of the questions prove to be valuable all the time, some most of the time, and some only now and then. The key questions are those that are valuable all the time. Each key question is listed and explained in the study guide (section 2). Knowing how the church functions on these questions is essential to any type of strategic thinking.

Approach the Ministry Audit as if it were a puzzle, which means that you want to put the pieces together. But this puzzle has no picture to guide your search. Wait until you have all the pieces of the puzzle in place before you make any decisions.

Don't get lost in the detail of the completed picture. Look at the big picture. The primary mistake that leaders make when planning is getting lost in details long before they map out any action plans.

Ready, Set, Go!

The steering team is in place. Copies of this workbook are in their hands. The Worship Survey has been administered for four consecutive weeks, and the data has been recorded on the master audit. The worksheets for the official administrative body and the paid staff have been administered and recorded on the master audit. Now you are ready to paint the big picture in section 2.

Section Two

THE STUDY GUIDE

THE BASIC LAW
OF CONGREGATIONAL LIFE

You will be my witnesses in Jerusalem, in all Judea and Samaria, and to the ends of the earth.

—ACTS 1:8b

Churches grow when they intentionally reach out to people instead of concentrating on their institutional needs. Churches die when they concentrate on their own needs.
This is the Basic Law of Congregational Life.

As a young boy, I was fascinated by the effect of throwing pebbles into a pond. One tiny pebble would produce an ever-widening circle that eventually filled the entire pond, and if I had thrown the stone near the center of the pond, when the ripple reached the bank it rippled back to the point where it had originated.

The church of Jesus Christ is like an ever-widening circle. As it gives itself away on behalf of others, it grows. Everything we do on behalf of others comes back to us. This is the way life works. We give and we receive.

One week, after preaching a sermon entitled "The Everwidening Circle," I received a note from a member of the church: "It's time for some sermons about personal and spiritual growth as well as institutional growth. We have some needs out here, too!"

The member missed the point of the sermon. Churches are healthiest when they reach out. Members are best nurtured when they nurture others. The art of giving has healing effects. Jesus taught us this in all he said and did: those who lose their lives will find them (Matt. 10:39). We have a need to help others. God made us that way. We find emotional and spiritual health by moving beyond concern for self.

The Biblical Basis

The Bible is filled with references to the Basic Law of Congregational Life, such as "love your neighbor as yourself" (Matt. 22:39). The most gripping reference may be when Jesus talked about this law in the commission that he left with his disciples in the upper room. He instructed them in the law when he said, "You will be my witnesses in Jerusalem, in all Judea and Samaria, and to the ends of the earth" (Acts 1:8*b*). Our Lord's last words are very clear—the mission of the church is to continually increase its ability to give itself away on behalf of all God's creation.

Examine the diagram of the ever-widening circle. The circles represent the life cycle of a church. It is the biblical affirmation that the farther a congregation moves from the center, the healthier the church becomes. The less of "you" and the more of God there is at the center of the circle, the healthier the congregation becomes.

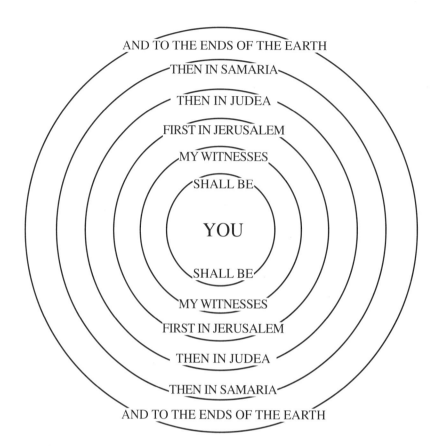

The third ring, "Jerusalem," represents a local congregation. One of the more common excuses given by both clergy and laity for avoiding church growth or evangelism is that churches should take better care of their present members before reaching out for more. But life doesn't work that way. The best way to nurture your members is to join them in reaching out to nurture someone else.

The fourth ring, "Judea," represents the geographic area that surrounds a local church. Every local church must feel a responsibility for an area larger than its own parish. The larger the area, the healthier the church will be.

The next ring, "Samaria," represents the unloved and unwanted people of our society. The Samaritans were the outcasts of Jesus' day, but Jesus said that the churches must reach out to include the present-day Samaritans.

The sixth ring, "the ends of the earth," represents world missions. A local church needs a vision for world missions that does not place a limit on its sphere of responsibility. For church growth with integrity, a church must really believe that with God's help, there are no limits to the scope of its ministry. The circle always must be growing wider.

The Argument

The Basic Law of Congregational Life is the basis for biblical ministry because it focuses on life's fundamental challenge: to overcome self-centeredness. Jesus asked us to be his witnesses, not our own. He asked us to move away from considering ourselves the center of our universe, to put others in our place. He knew that when we do so, we become healthy.

One Sunday after worship I received an anonymous note scribbled on the back of a registration card: "Who says our church has to grow? I think [our church] has grown enough." On another occasion, when I announced a series of sermons on the ever-widening circle, I received this note: "Please make it clear at the beginning that growth for growth's sake is not what you're talking about." At another time I was handed one that read: "I hope we're not trying to reach more new members just to fund the budget."

In most churches, growth is almost as difficult to talk about as money or politics. Why? Probably because we do not want to lose control of our own church; new people mean less control for ourselves. We are comfortable the way we are, and we do not like to change to accommodate new people and new ideas.

The Basic Law of Congregational Life is a reminder that life does not revolve around self. As a rule, twentieth-century Christians have not understood that life centers around our relationship with Christ and others, not around ourselves. We have viewed the mission of the church primarily in light of our own personal needs. We have failed to understand that we are made in such a way that our needs are nurtured best as we take care of the needs of others. When we talk about taking care of our own membership before being involved in evangelism or outreach, we reveal a lack of understanding of the mission of the church. The basic mission of the church is to help me nurture others; and in that process, I will be nurtured too!

Why Do Churches Grow and Die?

Allow me to introduce Joe. Joe has been married for ten years. He and his wife have two children: one is six years of age; the other, three months. Neither Joe nor his wife have been to church since they left their parents' homes. The oldest child is now ready to start school, and Joe's wife has decided it is also time for the children to receive a Christian education. Joe doesn't want to go to church, but he gives in because his wife insists.

The first obstacle Joe faces is a lack of convenient parking. By the time he gets to the church, he is irritated because he has had to walk a block. The second obstacle is the absence of directional signs to the nursery. No member of the church is willing to break away from a personal conversation to help Joe's family find their way. By now Joe is fuming.

Finally, Joe's family locates the sanctuary, only to sit shoulder-to-shoulder with a lot of strangers. Joe does not like to have strangers that close. He wants plenty of elbow room. As the service progresses, Joe is asked to hold up his hand so that everyone will know he is not a member. He does not want anyone to know he is there, much less that he is not a member.

Then without warning, the whole congregation suddenly rises and begins to sing something that all good Christians are supposed to know—the Doxology. Joe doesn't know the Doxology. The page number is printed in the bulletin, so he frantically finds the right place, only to realize that the song is over.

The sermon puts Joe to sleep because it talks about things he cannot apply to his daily life and it uses words with which he is not familiar. When the service is over, Joe and his family leave without being greeted by anyone. Later, Joe informs his wife that he does not intend to go through that torture again!

Now allow me to introduce Max. Max is a long-term member of the church Joe just visited. His children are all grown. He is a few years from retirement, and he has helped the church with several building programs. Max has been a member for so long he can't remember what it's like to be uncommitted to Christ and his church.

When told about Joe's reaction to his visit to the church, Max said, "If he isn't any more committed than that, let him stay at home. I don't mind walking a block to church. Besides, he's probably not willing to help pay for a new sanctuary anyway."

Christian churches are filled with good people like Max, and because of that, they are dying. Dying churches fail to remember that many of their present members were once just like Joe. They were not committed, and they could not have cared less about attending church. Today's world is filled with people like Joe—good people with families, but unchurched and uncommitted.

There is a world of difference between the value systems of Max and Joe. Max believes people should be as far out of debt as possible; Joe thinks the more credit he has, the more affluent he is. Max trusts institutions; Joe doesn't. Max serves God out of duty, obligation, and commitment; Joe serves out of compassion. Max has long-term plans and goals; Joe prefers instant gratification. Max married for life; Joe married in the hope that it would last. Max grew up in church; Joe did not. For growth to occur in mainline Protestant churches, Max must recognize the difference between his world and Joe's world.

Integrity Factors

Because there is always the danger that numbers and quantity can take prededence over a concern for people, any discussion about church growth must include enough integrity factors to avoid the possibility that quantity will become the primary emphasis of ministry. There are at least seven integrity factors present in healthy church growth:

1. People take precedence over institutional maintenance.
2. Ministry is balanced.
3. There is a high ratio between the membership and the number of people who attend worship.
4. There is a balance between money spent on the church and money spent on others.
5. A higher percentage of members join by profession of faith and restoration of vows than by transfer of membership.
6. Growth is stable and steady.
7. An inclusive faith is stressed.

These seven factors will be examined throughout this book.

The Basic Law of Congregational Life is that churches are healthiest when they reach out to others. Churches grow because they are intentionally concerned about the needs of others. Churches die because they concentrate primarily on their internal needs. With this law before us, we are now ready to explore the growth principles.

GROWTH PRINCIPLES ONE THROUGH SIX: MEETING PEOPLE'S NEEDS

Growth Principle One:
Meet the Needs of People
(Key Questions: 1, 2, 4-6, 9, 13, 14, 17)

Data Source: Worship Survey; Staff Worksheet, questions 1-8; Official Body Worksheet, questions 1-9

Question 1: What is the age, sex, and marital status of adult worshipers?

The information for answering question 1 comes from the Worship Survey that you took on four consecutive Sundays. When figuring average attendance, count the children who are present even if they do not attend worship. Just count the average number of children in Sunday school and add that to the worship average. If you are using the spreadsheet file from the bonus disk, retrieve "WRSHPENT.TXT" and print a report, so that you can port the data to the Ministry Audit.

The Four Generations

The ages are broken down into the four key generations as described by William Straus and Neil Howe in their book *Generations: The History of America's Future* (see Recommended Reading). They explore the cycle of generations in American history. They are the G.I. generation, the silent generation, the baby boom generation, the baby buster generation, and the millennial generation. By studying these generations a church can decide where to place its emphases.

People born from 1900 to 1924 make up the *G.I. generation.* The G.I. generation made up 8.4 percent of the national population in 1993 and will make up 7.3 percent in 1998. They made unprecedented progess in science, medicine, and the pursuit of individual liberties around the globe, especially as they overcame the tyranny and evil of two global wars which were sandwhiched around a massive economic depression. Now this generation feels that its values and acievements are under attack.

The challenge the church faces is how to help this generation surrender some of its hard-earned privileges for the good of others and the future. Faced with uncertainty about health and longevity, this group will now begin to deal with the fact that they no longer have a future that is more promising than the past, and the future they now see may be filled with uncertainty and threats. The act of losing their lives that they may find them will be a practical issue as they experience the loss of power and control over their lives, society, and the church.

People born from 1925 to 1945 make up the *silent generation*. The silent generation made up 15.2 percent of the national population in 1993 and will make up 12.7 percent in 1998. They feel caught between the G.I. generation and the baby boom generation. They seek to find compromises, try to balance the needs of aging parents and boomer children who have turned away from the values of their grandparents. Their inclination to find a middle ground between the two groups will not be appreciated by either group. They may serve as leaders in the 1990s, but this leadership will be short, as society and the church make the shift to baby boom generation leaders. The church must work hard to keep this age-group in order to have the benefits of its sense of fairness and compassion. This will not happen without effort on the church's part. The church will need to be sure that it is keeping some members of the silent generation in leadership positions.

People born from 1946 to 1964 make up the *baby boom generation*. This generation made up 28.1 percent of the national population in 1993 and will make up 24.1 percent in 1998. The boom generation will get attention. Its size makes it a key group for any congregation that is seeking to plan its future. This group will not be easy to work with as they turn their attention to reform the institutions in which they are members. The church will be no exception. Women will seek leadership and will not be satisfied to play a secondary role. The church will need to focus on societal issues. Abortion will be one of the key issues, and boomers will be on both sides and hold uncompromisingly to positions that will be difficult to reconcile.

Spiritual growth issues will remain high on their agenda. While family issues will be important to them, families will be more diverse than anytime before. This generation will see the fading of early retirement from their plans. They will be a healthier generation, and as their children grow up and move from home, boomers will travel and continue to seek experiences for growth. They will want experiences that make a contribution not only to others but to their own growth as well. They will begin to need help dealing with aging parents while rearing families that were begun later in life. They will feel tension between these two responsibilities. Day care services for the parents of the boomers may begin to be as important as day care is for their children today. Many of the women in this generation will be charting untested waters and will have little hope for help from the silent and G.I. generations. Women's concerns will become more important.

This generation will be looking for ways to recapture the collective experiences of their youth, and as the most educated generation in our history they will seek more opportunities to explore their own spiritual and intellectual growth and will find them in many novel and new ways. The challenge to the church is to contribute to this generation's maturation, so that they will be able to deal with their mortality and discover not only their need for grace but the need to be graceful toward others. It is hard today for a church to grow if it is not reaching baby boomers. My book *How to Reach Baby Boomers* discusses the challenges of that task in detail (see Recommended Reading).

People born from 1965 to 1982 make up the *baby buster generation*. The buster generation made up 30.6 percent of the national population in 1993 and will make up 30.1 percent in 1998. This generation presents a new challenge. One cannot assume that what has worked with the baby boom generation will work with the baby bust generation. Members of this generation will live their entire lives in the shadow of the boomers, and are facing a much less promising future than the boomers did at the same age. They are dealing with issues such as AIDS, a sluggish economy, governments having to raise taxes and cut benefits, and the elimination of many good blue- and white-collar jobs. Realism rather than idealism will be the mainstay of their lives. Practical concerns will be important to them. They will need help to confront the harsh realities that they will face their entire lives. They will be pragmatic, and this will be an important balance for the idealism of the boomers. The church will have to stay in close touch with these persons who will be in their late teens to early thirties in the 1990s. The church must now begin to focus serious attention on the busters.

"Twentysomething" adults are the primary target for church growth over the next thirty years. They will be even more important than baby boomers. The journey from eighteen into the thirties is a turbulent time of transition. Times of transition are the best times to reach people. However, many of this generation will have no church background, and thus they may not turn to the church in times of trouble. It is essential that the church find ways to reach out to them.

People born from 1983 to 2003 make up the *millennial generation.* The millennial generation in 1993 made up 17.7 percent of the national population, and in 1998 they will make up 25.4 percent. Since we are halfway through the birth years of this generation, we will see a significant increase in the number of children in this generation over the decade. We have already seen the first signs of interest in providing this generation with the best quality education, and that includes providing places of safety for learning in an increasingly violent world. There are also signs everywhere acknowledging that the needs of children have been ignored. Members of this generation will be rational doers, and the educational and emotional training we give them will steer them in that direction. This will be the decade for any and all programs for children and youth. This trend will continue in the first decade of the next century. It will pose important challenges to the church.

Interpreting the Worship Survey

With question 1 of the Ministry Audit, you will be calculating percentages that are based on the Worship Survey. The following steps explain how to fill in the blanks:

1. M/M = male married; M/S = male single; F/M = female married; F/S = female single.
   Calculate the percentages of respondents who fall within
   a. the four main age groups;
   b. the sixteen categories.

> **HINT: Add the percentages for the G.I. generation and the silent generation. The lower the combined percentage for these two generations, the better. If more than 50 percent of the worshiping congregation is over fifty years of age, it is more difficult for the congregation to minister to the unchurched. People between fifty and seventy years of age tend to resist change in their churches. The higher the percentage, the more urgent it is that you act strategically, and soon.**
>
> **In 1995, people fifty years old have a life expectancy of 29.1 years.**
>
> **In 1995, people sixty years old have a life expectancy of 20.9 years.**

2. In the far right column under question 1, note the gender and marital status of all the respondents to the Worship Survey.

> **HINT: On average, males make up 48 percent of attenders at churches in the U.S. If the proportion of males attending your church falls significantly below 38 percent, consider developing ministries for men.**

3. You can approximate the number of singles, separated, and divorced people in worship by counting the number of M/S and F/S people born between 1943 and 1961. Singles between those ages are probably single, separated, or divorced—not widowed.

Question 2: *Does our pastor understand the everyday world of our members?*

This is one of the key questions that deserves your special attention. (The score comes from the Official Body Worksheet—or "BODY1ENT.*" on the bonus disk—question 1.) The pastor must have a good image throughout the leadership before significant transformation can occur. Compare this answer with the leadership's answers to the questions about the pastor in growth principle 7, question 6; and growth principle 9, questions 2 and 7-17. There should be a close correlation between the response to this question and the responses to these other questions. If there is, the answers regarding the pastor are a reliable reading of how the leadership feels about the pastor; if there is not a close correlation, they are probably not reliable scores. Usually, the longer a pastor has been at a church, the lower and more positive the scores. Smaller churches that have had a turnover in pastors every year or so usually score higher than average (2.73).

Question 4: *Has there been any major controversy or division in the preceding five years?*

The most common conflicts I have encountered are (1) the adult choir does not cooperate, (2) the trustees exert far too much power in the decision-making process, (3) the finance committee or the financial secretary makes life miserable for anyone wanting to start a new ministry that costs money, and (4) there are one or two long-term members of the church who have no office in the church but must be consulted before any decision can be made. Has the congregation settled and resolved the conflicts? Unresolved corporate pain is one of the top ten reasons why churches do not reach the unchurched. If serious conflict from the past still haunts your congregation, it might be necessary to settle it before acting on any of the rest of the recommendations you might make.

Question 5: *Does our church deal openly with controversy?*

As you can see from the average score, it is not unusual for a significant number of people to feel as if their church does not deal openly with conflict. This often means that there are people in the church who feel stifled. Perhaps they have had new ideas turned down.

Questions 6, 9, 14, 17: *How do we make decisions?*

All four questions deal with aspects of the same issue. The goal is to have as flat an organization as possible and to make the decision-making process open and accessible to anyone. Are there several layers of administration? Are numerous meetings required before a decision can be made? Are most of the decisions on new proposals "NO"? If so, these are signs of decay and too much structure.

> **HINT: In question 14 of the Ministry Audit, look for comments such as "trustees" or "one or two people." The most effective churches have no more than one level of withholding permission. People should be able to start new ministries by approaching one central committee that can give an answer, rather than having to go through a labyrinth of committees. For more information on permission giving organizations, see my book *Sacred Cows Make Gourmet Burgers* (see Recommended Reading).**

Question 13: *What percentage of the total budget is devoted to programs?*

It is healthy for traditional, program-based churches to devote 10 percent of their budget to programming. (This does not apply to churches based on small groups in the meta model.)

Action Items for Meeting the Needs of People

1. Immediately begin new ministries specifically for young adults if more than 50 percent of the worshipers in your church were born before 1942.
2. Resolve any major conflict before attempting to start new ministries, unless the new ministries are the only way to resolve or do away with the conflict.
3. Consider restructuring if you have a lot of red tape or several layers of groups who withhold permission for new ministries. But remember that restructuring does not help a church unless that church has vision and is willing to act on a plan.
4. Call the Chamber of Commerce and tell them you are a pastor or church leader trying to find out more about your community. Ask if they can send you any demographic information they have concerning the population, projects, trends, age, gender, income, working habits, or any other social, religious, or economic issue in your area.

Growth Principle Two:
Give People Choices
(Key Questions: 1, 2, 5-15, 17-19)

Data Source: Staff Worksheet, questions 9-26; Official Body Worksheet, questions 10-11

Question 1: *Does our church offer a balanced ministry?*

One of the key features of the last part of the twentieth century is providing a wide variety of high quality choices. The more quality choices a church can provide for both churched and unchurched people the healthier the church will be.

Balance is the key. Churches that are committed to social justice have ministries that approach pain and injustice in two ways: (1) through social justice ministries, such as Habitat for Humanity, clothes closets, and homeless shelters, that address immediate needs; and (2) the root cause ministries, such as action groups that organize people to change the way economic decisions are made in your community or state. Consider this kind of ministry in light of growth principle 6. Churches need more high quality ministries in the mercy category than in the categories of love and justice combined, because more people are unchurched today than are churched. My estimates are that 75 to 80 percent of people under thirty years of age are unchurched (that is, either "pre-Christian" or not "committed Christians").

Question 2: *Does our church offer more than one Sunday morning worship service?*

The most important decision a church can make is to add a second worship service. I know of very few growing churches with one worship service. If you have just one service, look for ways to start a second, no matter how small you might be. The odds are that the present service is designed for people born before 1950. Make this second service very different from the present one. Usually, the addition of a worship service will increase the number of people hearing the gospel each week at your church by 12 to 20 percent in eighteen months.

Question 5: *Are we willing to have a worship service at the same time we have Sunday school?*

Holding worship and Sunday school at the same hour results in more people spending only one hour at your church on Sunday; in other words, most of the newcomers will opt for worship, not Sunday school. However, most of these people would never be in Sunday school anyway and would not be in worship without an additional service. This arrangement results in more young adults attending worship and leaving their children in the nursery or Sunday school. But don't worry about a worship service during the Sunday school hour hurting Sunday school attendance. It will not; in fact, it will increase it. Some people will go to worship instead of going home while their children are in Sunday school. In time, some will commit to two hours. Consider this idea in light of growth principle 8.

Questions 6, 7, 8, 9: Does our church offer weekday ministries for children?

A childcare program, run by the church as an extension of its children's ministry, is one of the easiest and most effective ways to reach into the homes of the unchurched. It provides a needed service, teaches values, and evangelizes as well.

Weekday ministries for children, including preschool, day care, Parents' Day Out, Parents' Night Out, kindergarten, or grade school, work best for the children, the parents, and the church if the ministries are considered an extension of the church. It is best if the person responsibe for the ministries is part of the church staff and is accountable either to the pastor or to the person who gives regular supervision of the church staff. The weekday children's ministries and the Sunday school need to work closely together so that most toys and equipment can be used by both. The budget needs to be set by the official body of the church and the curriculum needs to include religious training and offer chapel once a week. In most cases the ministries should not only be totally self-sustaining, but should also return 15 percent of their gross income to the church budget to help with other ministries that cannot sustain themselves, such as the children's Sunday school or a singles' ministry.

Have a parenting seminar for the parents. Put a monthly article from the program director in the newsletter. Put these families on your mailing list and send them the church newsletter. Once a year, have the children learn some songs and have them share the songs in worship. Their parents will attend. The person in charge of these ministries should work very closely with the pastor. The Sunday school teachers should understand the school to be a very important extension of the Sunday school and a major entry point into the lives of unchurched people.

This program is so basic that it is worth designing the building program around it, keeping in mind that you will need to use these facilities twenty years from now for elder care weekday ministries.

Questions 10, 15: How often do we start new Sunday school classes?

Sunday school classes more than six months old tend to be hard for new people to join. It's not that the classes are unfriendly, but that they have become close-knit families, and families do not take in new members easily. If you are a program-based church and are interested in cutting the inactive list, then establish new classes every six months. If you decide to develop a small group ministry around the meta model, you do not have to worry about starting new classes. For ideas on how to start new classes, see some of the resources listed in the Recommended Resources section under "Sunday School."

> **HINT: Most churches plateau because they do not have enough small groups that are open to new people; they reach the "single-cell ceiling." In other words, they have just enough small groups to care for the number of people presently attending. Small groups reach the saturation point and tend to become closed to new people when they (1) have been in existence for more than six months; (2) grow beyond eight people, and the purpose of the group is caring, sharing, and intimacy; (3) grow beyond fifteen, and the purpose of the group is task-achievement; (4) grow beyond thirty-five, and the purpose is fellowship.**

Question 11: How many adults attend Sunday school, in how many classes?

Equipping adults is the most important ministry in the church. Adults bring children; children seldom bring adults. Skill training is the most challenging adult ministry today. It is increasingly common for adults to lack skills in such basic areas as parenting, social graces, making friends, and interpersonal relations. Most adults today know very little about the Bible. Until they do, it is very unlikely that serious ministry will occur. There are several Bible studies that can begin the process of educating adults about the Bible (see "Bible Studies" and "Adults" in the Recommended Resources section).

The best Sunday school classes are small-group Bible studies with a focus on outreach, assimilation, and fellowship. Keep these classes small by starting a new class every time the class attendance averages fifteen or twenty, even if it means there will be more than one class for some age groups. Large classes are good for singles and for those born before 1950. Ask each class to set a goal of 5 to 15 percent growth and to report the percentages to the person in charge of Sunday school. Ask the Sunday school class to appoint a shepherd to call all of the first-time visitors. Consider using conference calls for Sunday school classes that wish to talk with a member of the class who has been absent or who is having a special day such as a birthday.

Question 12: How many singles attend Sunday school, in how many classes?

Three types of singles make up a singles' ministry: separated, divorced, and never married. Widows are not single and should not be combined with younger singles. Divorced or separated people consider themselves single, and tend not to feel comfortable in couples classes. Divorced people are the best candidates for singles' ministries. Those who have never been married usually see themselves as different from those who have been divorced. They often prefer to be included in couples' classes.

Do not start a singles' ministry unless you can devote a half-time paid person to the ministry. Singles' ministries require two or three nights of programming each week. One of these nights needs to be a relational event at which singles can meet one another. Usually the relational event is on Saturday night in the form of a "mixer." You can start a singles' ministry by doing the following: Develop a core group of singles. After you have started a singles' Sunday school class, have a city-wide stand-up buffet with good live music. Sell tickets in advance through the various singles' groups in town. Having people register for a door prize is a good way to get names and addresses to put on the mailing list. The only religious happening at such an event is to give them a handout about the new singles' Sunday school class that begins the next morning. Check the resources listed under "Singles" in the Recommended Resources section.

Question 13: How many youth attend Sunday school, in how many classes?

It is essential to have Sunday school classes for youth if you are a program-based church. It does not work well to combine junior high youth and senior high youth. Good youth programs seek to nurture the following strengths: (1) youth who avoid peers with negative behavior, (2) youth who are motivated and committed in school, (3) youth who are involved in structured activities, (4) youth who attend religious services, (5) youth who experience a caring and supportive school environment, and (6) youth who have caring and supportive families.

According to the Search Institute, a nonprofit group that studies trends in children and youth, nine factors help build a strong community that nurtures youth: (1) Church leaders should get to know the youth in the church by name and provide mentoring opportunities. Do the leaders stop in the hallways to talk with the youth? Do the youth have any say in the affairs of the church? (2) Church leaders should provide a positive vision for the youth. This is helped by the amount of good space given to the youth. Do they have their own room that they can decorate? Do they have enough space for more than just sitting around in a circle to hear a lesson? How much money is in the budget for the youth? Are retreats and outings planned? Is there a regular trip planned each year open only to those who have been in worship, Sunday school, and any evening youth program on three out of four Sundays? And do they have to raise most of the money spent on youth trips? (3) Parents should be involved in the youth program instead of the youth worker simply taking care of the youth. If you have a youth worker, that person should understand that he or she is working primarily with families who have youth and not just the youth. (4) The church should provide for all types of youth activities—athletics, music, drama, and so on. The goal is not to involve busy youth in yet another round of activities, but to provide appropriate enriching activities for all young people. (5) Churches need to support other organizations dedicated to youth. (6) Children and youth should be a top priority of the church. They should not get the leftovers, such as old couches and broken furniture. Their rooms should be some of the best in the church. (7) The church should encourage the youth to be visible in worship from time to time. (8) Facilities should not be better cared for than the youth. The congregation should be concerned more about the youth than about keeping the facilities clean. (9) The church should have clear-cut policies, actively and consistently put into place and lived out by those who work with the youth, on alcohol, drugs, movies shown at the church, adult behavior, and so on. Check the resources listed under "Youth" in the Recommended Resources section.

> **HINT:** According to the Harvard Educational Letter, the only meaningful categories of significant networks for youth moving from junior high to senior high are athletics, cheerleading, or being a friend of either an athlete or a cheerleader. A youth choir can provide a needed alternative. One way to build a youth choir is to plan a youth choir tour to some part of North America for a week. In order to go on the trip the youth must sing on three out of four Sundays the previous year and raise a large portion of their cost for the trip.

Question 14: How many children attend Sunday school, in how many classes?

It is best to keep all elementary grades separate and even to have a class for children who turned six too late to enroll in school. It is best to have a male and a female teacher. Male teachers can make an important contribution to the lives of children who do not have male role models at home. Most children learn better today through computers than through print. Put three or four computers in the children's Sunday school area and obtain some good Bible software. Arrange a schedule that will allow all the classes to use the computers. Check the Recommended Resources section under "Children and Computers."

Question 17: Does our church have midweek programs?

A major change during the past twenty years has been the increasing demand for seven-day-a-week churches. A healthy program-based church will have two to three people on the property during the week for every one person in worship on Sunday. Read Lyle Schaller's book *The Seven-Day-A-Week Church* (see Recommended Reading).

Often churches with less than three hundred in worship fail to develop core ministries. Core ministries are those ministries that are as important to continue as worship and Sunday school. These ministries are carried over from layperson to layperson, clergy to clergy. A core ministry is anything that is considered so important that no matter who the pastor is or what the skill level of the laity is, the program continues. As they grow, program-based churches often fail to expand their number of core ministries that bring new people into a relationship with the church, they stop meeting the needs of people, and they stagnate.

In 90 percent of United States communities, people between twenty-eight and forty-five are the largest segment of the population as well as the largest unchurched adult group. We know several important things about these people: (1) They do not trust institutions and have rejected the institutional church. (2) They are morally adrift but are wanting help finding an anchor for themselves and their children. (3) They resist rules but respond to reason. (4) They have many legitimate questions about faith and Christianity. (5) They want an experience more than values and beliefs. (6) They are not joiners but are looking for a place to belong—a place for relationships. (7) They distrust authority but respond to personal mentoring and role-modeling. (8) They are not loyal to denominations but respond to churches that meet their needs. (9) They are tolerant of others' beliefs but expect their spiritual leaders to know where they stand and what they believe. (10) They may attend church if a friend invites them, but they often do not stay because the worship is boring. (11) They want anonymity. (12) They look for quality. (13) They expect "how to" and "so what" sermons. (14) They do not like "holier than thou" sermons.

The most helpful thing you can do to determine which new ministries to begin and which ones to drop is to conduct a demographic study of your ministry area. Concentrate on an area five to ten miles around your church. If you do not have access to a Percept demographic report (check under "Demographics" in the Recommended Resources section), make sure questions 8 and 9 under growth principle 15 of the Ministry Audit have been filled out. You can gather demographic information about your area by calling the Chamber of Commerce or by ordering a demographic study from Church Information Development Services.

Telemarketing can be used in establishing new ministries in three ways: to discover what needs exist, to test the need for an already determined ministry, or to announce the beginning of a program. You can use it either to announce a new ministry or to gain information about future ministries. A call might go something like this: "I'm Jane Doe from X Church. Could I have thirty seconds to ask you one question?" If the person answers yes then ask, "If our church provided a quality kindergarten, would you be interested in receiving information about the programs?" If the person answers yes, then say, "Thank you so much for your time. We'll put you on our mailing list and keep you informed on what our church does with this information." If the answer is no, then say, "Thanks so much for your time. If we can ever be of any help to you or your family, please call us. Our church is in the Yellow Pages under. . . . " Check the resources listed under "Telemarketing" in the Recommended Resources section.

Focus groups can also help you determine which new ministries to begin. These groups need to be made up of either very new members (who have been members for no longer than one year) or unchurched people in the neighborhood. See the Recommended Resources section—"Demographics" 4, 5, and 6.

Question 18: *Does our church have Bible studies?*

Weekday Bible study is essential today because the unchurched are on a spiritual journey. If the emphasis is on content, Bible study works best when it is done in large groups led by the pastor. If the emphasis is on changing lives, then it is best done in small groups led by laypeople. Both emphases are essential.

Question 19: *Does our church have athletic programs?*

Athletics led by the church and seen as avenues into people's lives are another way to reach the unchurched. The leaders, however, have to understand that the purpose of the program is bring people closer to one another and to God, not to win.

Action Items for Giving People Choices

1. Based on your demographic study (if you have one), decide which new outreach ministries to begin and which ones to strengthen.
2. If you have only one adult class on Sunday, begin a second one.
3. If you have a weekday children's ministry that pays rent, find a way to replace it with one that your church runs. Make it distinctively Christian.

Growth Principle Three:
Match People with Their Skills
(Key Questions: 1, 2)

Data Source: Staff Worksheet, questions 27, 28

Question 1: What is our nominating process?

Most nominating groups are too small. It is best if the nominating group includes one person for every twenty-five people in worship.

Question 2: Do we encourage and use spiritual gift inventories?

The emphasis is on how God made us, not what the institutional church needs us to do. Discovering spiritual gifts is more important than time and talent surveys that are dependent on people having some experience working in the church. Spiritual gifts are explained in detail in my book *Sacred Cows Make Gourmet Burgers* (see Recommended Reading).

Action Item for Matching People with Their Skills

Consider ways to use spiritual gifts or enlarge the nominating committee so that there is one person for every twenty-five people in the average worship service.

Growth Principle Four:
Prevent Inactives
(Key Questions: 1, 2, 4-8 12)

Data Source: Staff Worksheet, questions 29-40

Question 1: What is our membership trend?

Although membership does not mean much to people born after 1950, it is a helpful tool to describe the future of the church twenty-five years from now. Based on the past ten years, what will the membership be twenty years from now if it continues on the present path?

Question 2: What are our losses?

Concentrate on the number of deaths. Is the number growing? Does it equal or surpass the numbers of transfers or withdrawals? Many churches find themselves getting so old that it takes more and more of the pastor's time simply to bury the church members or visit them in homes. A point is reached where there is little time left to reach the unchurched after providing spiritual and physical hospice care. In the book of Acts, Stephen and others are set aside to care for the widows and orphans so that the apostles can be about the primary work of the church—reaching the unchurched. This means that although no one should be overlooked or uncared for, the hospice needs of a congregation should not be the primary responsibility of the pastor or key laypeople.

Questions 4, 5, 12: *Are we assimilating?*

Studies show that 80 percent of the people who drop out of the church do so within their first year. Three out of four people say they left the church because they did not feel wanted. Those who make seven or more friends within their first three months in a congregation rarely drop out. This means that people may come to the church for a variety of reasons, but they stay if they make friends. Friends are seldom made in worship. It takes a program-based church a minimum of twenty hours per month to assimilate people. For this reason, assimilation works best when a paid staff person is responsible for seeing that it is done but not necessarily for doing it. Recruiting volunteers is essential.

Questions 6, 7: *Do we have enough small groups?*

Most life-changing events occur in small groups of five to seven people. There are various types of small groups, but the most important are the recovery, support, learning (nurturing), and mission (ministry) groups. Very few denominational small groups such as the women's or men's groups are reaching people born after 1950. See "Lay Ministries" in the Recommended Resources section.

Question 8: *How many inactive families do we have?*

Inactives are seldom recoverable. It takes ten hours to recover an inactive for every hour it takes to reach an unchurched person. It is best to concentrate on preventing inactives with outreach ministries to your members and outreach ministries to the unchurched. I recommend working with the inactives only under the following circumstances: (1) when a church has a new pastor, (2) when the area has a projected decline in population, or (3) when a church has a very high number of inactives. Within a new pastor's first three months, it is helpful to invite all the membership, especially the inactives, to a catered dinner to meet the pastor. See "Inactives" in the Recommended Resources section.

Action Items for Preventing Inactives

1. Begin new groups if you do not have a small group for every fifteen people in worship. This is one of the most important issues facing your church.
2. Recruit using a volunteer or a paid staff person, devoting twenty hours per month to assimilating people.

Growth Principle Five:
Provide a Wider Outreach
(Key Question: 1)

Data Source: Staff Worksheet, question 41

Question 1: *How much money do we spend on causes outside our congregation?*

A goal for effective churches is to devote 15 to 25 percent of their budget to missions. A good portion of this amount needs to be for hands-on mission in which people can participate. Is the amount growing? Usually, the larger a church gets the more it can give to missions.

> **HINT: The United States is now one of the primary mission fields in the world. More of our money needs to go to the local mission field.**

Action Items for Providing a Wider Outreach

1. Look for ways to put more money into hands-on ministries if the amount designated for such ministries is below 15 percent of your budget.
2. Seek a balance between your passion for sending money away to missions and your passion for strengthening your church and growing disciples.

Growth Principle Six:
Participate in the Public Arena
(Key Questions: 2, 3)

Data Source: Staff Worksheet, question 42; Official Body Worksheet, questions 12, 13

Healthy churches include basic social justice ministries, such as Habitat for Humanity or the local homeless shelter. However, I never recommend starting a serious justice ministry that attacks the root causes of injustice unless the pastor has been at the church for at least seven years. By then the pastor is trusted enough to not get kicked out when conflict occurs.

Social justice ministries, whether they address immediate needs or root causes, will be very important in the first part of the twenty-first century in reaching and discipling the baby buster generation. Avoid getting caught up in making official resolutions about issues. Resolutions are usually useless. All they do is make some people feel good about not being able to do anything about justice.

One of the finest social justice ministries in the United States is the Industrial Areas Foundation, which carries on the work of Saul Alinsky. This group is only for those churches that are serious about attacking the root causes of social injustice and empowering all levels of the social strata. Leadership development is the primary tool used by this group to organize people to deal with social injustice. I spent nine years being trained by them, and it was the finest education I have ever had in my ministry. To see if an Industrial Areas Foundation organization is in your area, call their San Antonio office at (512)222-8562.

Action Items for Participating in the Public Arena

1. Consider a serious social justice ministry only if your pastor has been with you for more than seven years.
2. Make partnerships with highly visible political personalities in the community. Give an award to an outstanding public servant and invite the civic leader to your church as a commitment to your cause.

GROWTH PRINCIPLES SEVEN THROUGH ELEVEN: WORSHIP, LEADERSHIP, AND ABILITY

Growth Principle Seven:
Emphasize Worship
(Key Questions: 1, 2, 6, 10, 11, 13, 15-17)

Data Source: Staff Worksheet, questions 43-50; Official Body Worksheet, questions 14-23

Questions 1, 2: *How important is worship?*

Worship is the most important thing a human being does. Without worship, the church is nothing. Worship is a better barometer of a church's health than membership. People can join and never be discipled. People can attend without joining and still be discipled. Count your worship attendance more than your membership.

It is important to be intentional about people joining your church. Those churches who allow people to join every Sunday need to leave about seven minutes for this part of the service. If your church allows people to join only at certain times, you need to make certain you are not asking them to join only when it is convenient for you. Be intentional about setting time aside each month for people to join. Look for ways to make joining the church an important step. It is all right to raise your standards for joining.

Senior pastors in churches with more than four hundred in worship need to be in the pulpit on forty-four to forty-six Sundays a year. This does not mean that the senior pastor has to preach all the services. Many churches have more than one preacher on the weekend (including Sunday).

Question 6: *Do the sermons speak to our personal needs?*

If the pastor's sermons are not practical enough to speak to people's personal needs, the church will have a hard time growing. It complicates matters even further if the pastor has no idea what unchurched people need. We are on a mission field today; we must meet people's basic needs first, and then we can introduce them to Christ. Perhaps the pastor needs to read some books on unchurched people, such as George Hunter's *How to Reach Secular People* (See Recommended Reading).

Question 10: *Is our worship music pleasing to a majority of the congregation?*

Obviously, most people in the church are comfortable with the music, or they would not be there. The key is to see if their response falls within the norm toward the positive side. If not, you should pay close attention to why they are not happy. Compare this score with growth principle 8, question 7.

Question 11: *What is the size of adult and youth choirs?*

If a choir sings in a service, the choir needs to include one person for every ten people attending that service. Music today is just as important as the sermon. If contemporary praise teams are used, each person needs to have a microphone.

The National Endowment for the Arts asked the census bureau to ask the public, "What are the three top types of music you listen to?" The results were as follows: country, 51.7 percent; easy listening, 48.8 percent; rock, 43.5 percent; rhythm and blues, 40.4 percent; big band, 35.5 percent; jazz, 34.2 percent; classical, 33.6 percent; show tunes, 27.8 percent; contemporary folk, 23.1 percent; opera, 12.6 percent. There were two problems with this survey. First, the survey allowed respondents to list only three types of music. Second, the survey did not include Christian music as an option. Christian music was the fastest growing segment of the music industry in 1995.

Question 13: *What is the percentage of worship attendance to membership?*

The average percentage for all size churches is 39 percent. For churches under two hundred in worship, 60 percent. For churches between two hundred and four hundred in worship, 45 percent. For churches over five hundred in worship, 28 percent.

Question 15: *What is our worship growth pattern?*

This is one of the most important barometers of the church's health. There are four types of worship attendance patterns: yo-yo, declining, stable, or growing. In a church with a *yo-yo* pattern, the worship attendance goes up and down from year to year, usually peaking and bottoming out at the same basic levels. Determine if there is a pattern with the yo-yo. Do the tops and the bottoms of the yo-yo seem to be close to the same number every time? Yo-yo churches tend to have one of three problems. Either they have reached or surpassed the 80 percent of capacity limit—in worship or in parking; or they have too many people attending for the number of paid staff; or they have had pastoral changes at the point of the peak or the decline. I will discuss these problems later.

If worship attendance at your church is *declining,* it is important to ask several questions: Why are we declining? Are we content with this situation? What can we do to stop it? Are we willing to pay the price? Stopping a decline usually means new staff and new ministries. Draw an imaginary line into the future following the downward direction of the worship attendance figures. Allow the impact of this to visually create a sense of crisis. What is going to happen to us if we do not do something?

In a church with a *stable* worship attendance pattern the fact that the church is holding its own can be deceiving. Even though the attendance is the same as it was ten years ago, the odds are that most of the people in worship are ten years older. This means that the church is traveling along the top of a mesa, where worship attendance will eventually just fall off the edge.

If your church's worhip attendance is *growing,* don't rest at ease in Zion. If it ain't broke, fix it. Are we willing to anticipate the future? How can we improve what we are doing? What new ministries do we need to begin? What programs no longer seem to be needed?

Question 16: How much money is budgeted for worship?

Spending money to improve the quality of music is the best money you will spend in today's world.

Question 17: Is our worship a form of drama?

To say worship is drama means that we understand that worship must move with the same flow and momentum as good drama. Worship does not have to be boring to be effective. To determine if your service flows well, record your service on audiotape and get into a quiet room, shut the door, play the tape, close your eyes, and count the number of times there is no sound for more than five seconds. If there is more than one, your service does not flow well, even if the silence is during the prayer time.

Videotape your service and compare it with MTV programming. It might be good for your worship leaders to gather each weekend before worship to go through the mechanics of the service. The more contemporary the service, the more important it is to do this.

Action Items for Emphasizing Worship

1. Work out a schedule for your senior pastor to be in the pulpit forty-four to forty-six Sundays per year. If you have associate pastors who want to preach, they can do so if you have two preachers each Sunday. This will give people a choice. This is very easy to do when you have three services.
2. Bring the membership in the choirs up to one person in the choir for every ten people in the average attendance at each service.
3. Provide a choir for each service and do not discontinue the choir's participation during the summer.
4. Set a goal to increase the ratio of the worship attendance to the membership by 10 percent over the next five years. Do not attempt to do this simply by cleaning the membership roles.
5. Decide what type of church you are and why you think you have this particular pattern.

Growth Principle Eight: Add a Worship Service (Key Questions: 1, 3-10, 12)

Data Source: Staff Worksheet, questions 51-61; Official Body Worksheet, questions 24-25

Questions 1, 4: How many worship services do we offer?

Anytime there is only one service, one of the most important things a church can do is start another service that is different from the existing service. It does not matter how empty the present worship service might be. The present worship service probably is traditional and will not meet the needs of most people in the changing world.

Morning worship services that begin at 8:00 or 8:30 seldom reach many people, and usually when they do the people are over fifty years of age. The best time to start another service is during Sunday school, between 9:00 and 10:00. There are at least ten important things to consider when starting an additional service.

1. Do not start a new service identical to what already exists. Instead decide on one of three target audiences: busters (people born between 1965 and 1982), boomers (people born between 1946 and 1964), or seniors (people born before 1946). Each requires a different style of worship. Identify the key issues in the target audience

(Do they see church as an option? When would they most likely attend? Why don't they attend now?). Focus groups with the appropriate age range can help you obtain this information.

2. Agree on the purpose for starting this new service. Make a statement of purpose that is measurable, theological, achievable, and controllable. If the service is different from what exists, refer to it as an addition, not a change. Introduce the service as an experiment that will be evaluated regularly.

3. Design the service to address the needs of the target audience. Do not plan it with the preferences of the present church members in mind.

4. Determine the time and place for the service. The fastest growing time period in North America for worship is between 9:00 and 10:00 A.M. When you have multiple services, it is okay to have worship and Sunday school running at the same hour (it will not hurt Sunday school attendance). If you do not already have three worship services on Sunday, put the service on Sunday morning. Weekday or Saturday services are much harder to establish than Sunday services. However, they will reach a different audience.

5. Spend at least six weeks communicating to your service area that you are starting this new service. This can be done through direct mail, announcements in the bulletin, radio, and so on. It is a mistake to start an additional service without telling the community. A good way to start such a service is to begin on the first Sunday in January and make a special invitation in the Christmas Eve services. Another good time to begin a new service is the second Sunday in September. In resort areas or in cold country, summer is a good time to initiate a new service.

6. Give the experiment at least a year's trial period before making any evaluations.

7. Make sure you have adequate leadership for whatever style of worship you intend to start. Multiple services are very hard on musicians, especially if they are being asked to develop an alternative style of worship. In some cases it is unfair to ask the current staff to provide a totally different service of worship. Additional part-time staff may be necessary.

8. If your target audience is busters or boomers, do not start the service until you have provided excellent child care and nursery facilities.

9. Be certain to have in place all the new support ministries you will need, such as ushers, greeters, a choir, and so on.

10. Put a follow-up procedure in place for guests. When the average score on question number 7 (Do we provide music of high quality?) is above 2.60, the congregation is telling you that they do not like the type of music in the worship service. Question 4 simply helps us understand how difficult it might be for the leadership to start another service, especially if the present one is not uncomfortably full.

Question 3: *When was the newest service started?*

It is usually effective to allow a new service to have eighteen months to develop before starting another service.

Questions 5, 7: *Does each service have a regular choir and music of high quality?*

In a traditional church it is essential to have a separate choir for every worship service. Do not rotate the choirs or allow a service to exist without its own choir. Rotation between services is hard on old habits. It is good to allow adults to sing at two services if they wish. In a nontraditional church it does not matter if there is a choir. It is essential that if there is a group or ensemble that leads worship each member has a microphone.

Questions 8, 10: *On how many Sundays each year does our adult choir sing?*

Healthy churches that have choirs do not cancel their regular choirs in the summer. When relocating, most persons move near the end of the school year, and after getting settled they start looking for a church in July and August or on Christmas Eve night. The number one time unchurched young families and singles go to church is Christmas

Eve. Easter is not nearly as fertile a field for reaching the unchurched as Christmas Eve. In anticipation of holiday travel, many churches have shut down their systems after the choral presentation the Sunday prior to Christmas Eve. In a similar manner, a signal is given to people when the church cuts back on their programs during the summer. When churches reduce their schedules during the summer, they tell people that it is okay to take a vacation from the organized Body of Christ. This translates to many that faith is not really the most essential part of our life. Unless the church presents faith (experienced in the worship of God) as the most important aspect of our lives, persons born after 1950 do not take the church seriously. Continue worship at the same hours during the summer. Continue Sunday school during the summer. Continue the choir during the summer. The adult choir should sing even when the children's choirs sing. If you live in a warm climate, air-condition at least the sanctuary.

Question 9: How many musicals, cantatas, or dramas does our choir present each year?

The more high-quality musical programs a choir performs, the better. Most healthy churches present at least two major musical programs per year. Contemporary churches find that concerts are an effective way of reaching into the lives of young adults. These do not have to be presented on Sundays and can include all types of music.

Question 12: How many Christmas Eve services does our church offer?

As I have already noted, Christmas Eve is one of the most important days of the year. Often, more first-time visitors will attend on this night than on any other day of the year. Send out a Christmas card to every home within a thirty minute drive from the church inviting them to the Christmas Eve services. The most popular times for worship on Christmas Eve night are 5:00, 7:00, 9:00, and 11:00. Candlelight is advised. Families with children might be encouraged to attend at 4:30 or 5:00 (let the children present a musical); a contemporary service may be offered at 7:00; a candlelight service with communion may be held at 9:00; and a traditional service may be offered at 11:00. In most areas the 11:00 service is waning in attendance.

Action Items for Adding Worship Services

1. If you have only one service, add one that is different from the present one. Focus on the largest adult age group in the area within ten miles of the church.
2. If your largest service on Sunday morning is 80 percent full, start another service on Sunday morning no matter how many services you have on Sunday morning.
3. If you are a traditional church and do not have a regular choir in an existing service, develop one for that service.
4. If your choir does not sing every Sunday in each service, then ask them to do so.
5. Plan as many concerts each year as your music department is able to do with quality.
6. If any of your present Christmas Eve services are 80 percent full, add another Christmas Eve service.

Growth Principle Nine:
Value the Leadership Strength of the Pastor
(Key Questions: 3-5, 7-17)

Data Source: Staff Worksheet, questions 62-64; Official Body Worksheet, questions 26-40

Questions 3-5: Do we experience long pastorates?

The average pastoral tenure in growing churches in the twenty-first century will be fifteen to twenty years. The same will be true for staff. When there is a match between the pastor or staff members and the church, encourage the pastor and staff to stay. The longer the pastor and staff stay, the more time away they will need for reflection and personal growth.

Questions 7-17: Is our pastor a leader?

For the relevant data, see questions 26 to 40 on the Official Body Worksheet (on the bonus software disk, this file is "BODY1.*"). The average among two hundred churches surveyed of the scores for questions 7-17 is 2.30. If you compare the average of these scores with the scores on growth principle 1, question 8 and growth principle 7, question 6, they should be within .50 in either direction to be reliable.

I have never seen a church whose transforming vision began with someone other than the pastor. I am sure it happens, but I think it is rare. In growing churches the pastor and staff must take the laity where they would not go on their own. Mistakes are inevitable when churches are traveling into new areas. Pastors must delegate everything possible. The more they delegate, the more laity blossom and the more people are reached for Christ. Some pastors are very effective in a church of one size and not effective in a church of another size. This is because churches of different sizes need different types of leadership skills. The world into which we are moving will be a diverse world of choices. To reach this world, pastors will have to be able to converse with a wide variety of lifestyles and value systems without feeling threatened. The ability to mediate between generations is essential. If the composite score of these answers is .50 above the average, ask why.

Action Items for Valuing the Leadership Strength of the Pastor

1. If there is a match between your pastor and the church and if your pastor has the talent or has or is willing to develop the skills to lead the church, what do you need to do to keep the pastor for fifteen to twenty years? Is this possible?
2. Provide a minimum of $1,500 in your budget per program staff person for continuing education.
3. If you are a traditional church, provide one program staff person for every one hundred people in worship, including children.
4. If the pastoral scores are way out of the norm to the negative side, encourage your pastor to work on his or her skills; however, make sure that a handful of people did not drive up the average by marking 10 on all the scores.

Growth Principle Ten:
Value a Growth-Oriented Attitude Among the Paid Staff
(Key Questions: 1, 2, 6, 7, 9, 11, 18-20)

Data Source: Official Body Worksheet, questions 41-45; Staff Worksheet, questions 65-79

Question 1: What is the main responsibility of the paid staff?

Healthy churches do not pay staff to do ministry. They should equip the laity to do ministry. Staff do not replace volunteers. Staff identify laity for ministry, recruit and deploy laity into ministry, and equip laity for ministry.

> **HINT:** Do not hire a youth director to lead the youth group and teach youth classes. Hire a youth director to recruit and train laypeople to lead and teach the youth group. Most program people should be able to pay for themselves within two to three years in additional people they bring into the church. If you have the right staff in the right ministry, you will have all or most of the volunteers you need.

Question 2: *How many paid staff do we have?*

The goal in a traditional church is to have the equivalent of one full-time paid program person for every hundred people in worship (including children, even if they are not in worship). More staff is needed today than in the 1950s because the world we live in today is far more complicated. In the 1950s, the nuclear family of Mom, Dad, and the kids came to church. Today, there are many types of families. In the 1950s, the church had very little competition for the lives of children and youth. Today, the church finds itself competing with a variety of things that pull children and youth away from the church. In the 1950s, the Judeo-Christian value system was reinforced in the home, the schools, and the church. Today, only the church reinforces the Judeo-Christian value system. Drugs and gangs were not nearly as widespread in the 1950s as they are today. Today, people are more mobile than they were in the 1950s and most often do not have an extended family nearby to help in times of crisis. In other words, it is far more difficult today than it was in the 1950s to minister to people and to equip them for a life that follows Jesus Christ.

Program staff includes the pastor and any paid staff members who work directly with people, with the exception of part-time musicians, who are support staff. Music directors are considered program people only if they are the equivalent of full-time and are constantly increasing the number of people involved in the church's music programs. Program staff should be able to function, most of the time, on their own with minimal input from the senior pastor. The primary role that the senior pastor should play is that of a visionary, not a nuts-and-bolts kind of leader. The larger the church, the truer this is. Support staff includes the organist, the pianist, any children's choir leaders, all handbell players, secretaries, custodians, administrators, business managers, and so on. If the area around your church is highly populated, it is not necessary to be able to afford the staff when you hire them. If you have enough money to pay them for one year, and you get the right staff, they should be paying their way in one and a half years.

Count your present program and support staff in terms of total full-time staff members. (For example, two half-time staff members equal one full-time staff member.)

Questions 6-7: *How do the pastor and the staff relate?*

If the scores from questions 42-43 on the Official Body Worksheet are over 3.10, investigate the relationship between the pastor and the staff.

Questions 9, 11, 18, 19: *How are staff meetings managed?*

These questions are important only if you have the equivalent of more than two full-time people on staff. The primary role of the senior pastor in multiple staff settings is to cast vision. See chapter 7 of *Sacred Cows Make Gourmet Burgers* (see Recommended Reading). Staff meetings need to be held weekly or daily for short periods of time. The larger the staff, the more important retreats become. Poor time management is rampant in church staffs. Most cities have short-term business courses on time management. If these are too expensive, see if you have a member who either teaches time management or knows someone who could volunteer to come in and work with the staff.

Question 20: *What teaching ministries do we have?*

In traditional churches it is important for the pastor to be a role model, emphasizing the importance of adult education by teaching regularly in the church school and weekly in a weekday Bible study.

In nontraditional churches it is important for all staff to teach in one or more settings by (1) attending or leading a weekly small group for Bible study, prayer, and sharing; (2) being part of a teaching church ministry that invites other churches to attend a seminar given by your church to learn how ministry is working in your church; (3) teaching a weekday Bible study. Presently, there are more adults in Bible study during the week than there are on Sunday.

Action Items for Encouraging a Growth-Oriented Attitude Among the Paid Staff

1. Pay staff only to *equip* laity to do ministry and then get out of the way. If you are paying staff to *do* ministry, you may need to compose new job descriptions.
2. If you are a traditional church, add enough staff to equal one staff person for every one hundred people in worship. If you are a nontraditional church, hire enough staff to equal one full-time person for every one hundred in worship up to two hundred in worship and then one for every two hundred thereafter.
3. Before hiring, have a clear picture of where your church is going and how this new staff will help you get there.

Growth Principle Eleven:
Think Clearly and Positively About Your Congregation's Size and Ability
(Key Questions: 1-16)

Data Source: Staff Worksheet, questions 80-82; Official Body Worksheet, questions 46-60

Question 1: *Are we small, medium, or large?*

Most churches do not realize how large they really are compared to other churches. The more clearly they understand their comparable size, the easier it is for them to take bigger steps of faith.

Questions 2-3: *What is our perception of our size?*

These two questions give you a reality check on how the leadership perceives the size of the church. Comparing the answer to question 2 with the answer to question 1 will show you how accurate or inaccurate your leadership's perception is.

Questions 4-15: *How is our lay leadership functioning?*

The composite average of all the scores for questions 4-15 is 4.1. You will notice this is higher (more negative) than the average of the scores evaluating the pastor's leadership. (I've never seen a church where the scores for the laity were lower than those for the pastor; if your church is an exception, please call me!) This means that laity do not appreciate their own skills as much as they do their pastor's. If you want your church to grow, the laity need to understand that they have incredible spiritual gifts to offer to the Body of Christ. Raising the leadership's understanding of their importance to actual ministry is essential. As churches grow, leadership requires a considerable amount of training in order to keep up with the accompanying dynamics of growth. Leaders in small churches operate differently than leaders in a large church. For example, personnel committees can evaluate a pastor, but it is impossible for them to evaluate three or four staff people they never observe on the job. As the church grows, it is best if the pastor evaluates the rest of the staff or if the staff evaluate one another. Trustee committees can handle property issues in a small, Sunday-only church. In a larger, seven-day-a-week church, it is impossible for trustees to care for the property in a timely fashion.

All finance and trustee people will benefit from a good, solid training session on the best way to be good stewards of the foundation money in light of the different ways in which baby boomers and busters approach the subject of money. An excellent book is Lyle Schaller's *44 Ways to Increase the Financial Base of Your Church*. In churches with over two hundred in worship, personnel and finance people will benefit from reading Lyle Schaller's *The Larger Church and the Multiple Staff. The Abingdon Guide to Funding Ministry* is an outstanding almanac for good stewards. *Giving and Stewardship in an Effective Church*, by Kennon Callahan, is also excellent. (See Recommended Reading.)

Question 16: How long do lay leaders lead?

It is best to limit the tenure of people holding office to three years to avoid power blocks within the decision-making process and to avoid burnout among people who are not power hungry. Also, such problems are less likely to occur among those people who are truly exercising their spiritual gifts.

Action Items for Improving Perception of Ability

1. Provide training sessions for lay leaders.
2. If your composite average for the scores to questions 4-15 on the Ministry Audit falls above 4.45, you need to work on leadership development and conflict management (conflict management only if (1) your composite average is above 4.55, (2) the answer to question 12 under growth principle 1 is yes, and (3) the answer to question 13 is above 5.4).
3. Have your church members read Lyle Schaller's *The Larger Church and the Multiple Staff* (see Recommended Reading).
4. I recommend that all lay leaders read the following books: William M. Easum, *Dancing With Dinosaurs* and *Sacred Cows Make Gourmet Burgers;* Lyle E. Schaller, *The Seven-Day-A-Week Church*; Loren Mead, *The Once and Future Church*; George S. Hunter III, *How to Reach Secular People* and *Church for the Unchurched* (see Recommended Reading).

GROWTH PRINCIPLES
TWELVE THROUGH SIXTEEN:
SPACE, DISTANCE, AND VISITORS

Growth Principle Twelve:
Provide Plenty of Space
(Key Questions: 1, 3, 4, 6-12)

Data Source: Staff Worksheet, questions 83-95; Official Body Worksheet, questions 61, 62

Question 1: *What level of commitment do we expect?*

A high level of commitment is one of the key factors I see in every growing congregation. God does not honor leadership that is half-committed. If the majority of your leadership does not answer "High," you need to raise your church's expectations concerning commitment level. This begins with a deeper appreciation of what it means to be a servant of Jesus Christ and of the absolute uniqueness of what the Christian church has to offer. Among the staff and key lay leaders is where this deeper commitment must begin. Usually, the problem lies with staff and laity who feel entitled to grace and do not act as role models of commitment.

Question 3: *How much space can we use?*

Anytime any facility is 80 percent full, it is time to provide more space. It is next to impossible to sustain growth beyond the comfort level of 80 percent capacity. This applies to everything the church does. The 80 percent rule is an invisible but powerful presence that works like the law of gravity. No one will tell you they are not coming back because the sanctuary or nursery or parking lot or Sunday school class is more than 80 percent full. In fact, no one really notices that the space is 80 percent full. It just feels uncomfortable. In the western states, the comfort level can be as low as 75 percent.

Question 4: *Do we need more worship space?*

Anytime your main worship service is 80 percent full, growth is seldom sustained over a two year period without adding another service or more space. If you do not do this, nothing else will matter. Consider this: It is immoral to continue to allow people to join the church while your worship attendance average remains the same because the primary worship service is too full. The same is true for parking. Educate your leadership on this important item. If your worship attendance average has been up and down like a yo-yo over a ten year period, one of three things will be true: (1) you have had a new pastor at each high attendance point, (2) your largest worship service is at the 80 percent limit, or (3) your parking is at the 80 percent limit.

Question 6: *Do we need more space for the choirs?*

A full choir is good, but it does discourage people from joining the choir. Perhaps you need more choirs or you need to start that second or third service so that each service has its own choir.

Question 7: *Do we need more nursery space?*

The nursery needs to be the nicest room in the church. It also needs to be on the same level as the sanctuary. A paid sitter who recruits volunteers is essential. The nursery should be open anytime the church is open. Separate the cribbers, crawlers, and walkers. Provide the visitors with a small brochure on the nursery. In growing churches it is best to require identification from parents as they are leaving a child in the nursery. Some churches require parents or caretakers to leave their drivers' licenses. Remember that kidnapping by noncustodial parents is a major problem. Check the Recommended Resources section under "Nursery."

Question 8: *Do we need more education space?*

This question is important only for traditional churches. Small groups that meet in homes take the place or supplement Sunday school in nontraditional churches.

Questions 9-11: *Are the Sunday school classes full?*

If any classes are filled to over 80 percent capacity, rearrange the classes to avoid as much of the problem as possible. Often, churches have small groups of older people meeting in rooms much too large and large groups of younger people meeting in rooms much too small because the older groups have met where they are for a long time (they used to need the space). Classes that do not want to move to make room for more people to learn about God do not understand what it means to follow Christ. If there are no rooms available, consider having classes in the pastor's office, in the kitchen, in hallways, and wherever you can find space.

Question 12: *Do we offer satellite ministries?*

Satellite ministries can help growing churches that need space. Is there a vacant building nearby that the church can rent and use for some of its ministries?

If you are a traditional church, this is an extremely important barometer of your future. If you do not offer satellite ministries, or if you are offering fewer than you once did, your worship and membership is prone to decline. If you are a nontraditional church, this is no longer an important barometer.

Action Items for Providing Plenty of Space

1. If the commitment level is not high, step up the preaching and teaching on servanthood. Staff should be role models of higher commitment. I am not suggesting that the solution is simply that "staff should try harder";

rather, I am emphasizing how the staff's commitment affects a congregation's perceptions of its own ability.

2. If you are over the 80 percent mark in worship, the first step is to add another service or a larger sanctuary or both.

3. If your choirs are full, provide more choir space or assign one distinct choir to each worship service.

4. Make the necessary nursery changes indicated by your analysis under question 7. This is one of the most important and urgent changes to make.

5. If your Sunday school is too full, either add another service, build, or start a small group ministry that meets in homes. For small group material, see the resources listed under "Lay Ministries—Small Group Ministries" in the Recommended Resources section.

6. Find another location for Sunday school classes that are filled to over 80 percent of capacity.

Growth Principle Thirteen:
Provide Adequate Parking
(Key Questions: 1-9)

Data Source: Staff Worksheet, questions 96-102; Official Body Worksheet, questions 63-64

Question 1: Does our church own enough land?

A minimum amount of land for a church in the twenty-first century is ten acres. Most churches planning on effective ministry are purchasing over thirty acres. If you plan to persist as a regional church, you must have eight acres. If you plan on being a megachurch (10,000 or more in worship) you need at least sixty acres.

Questions 2-9: How many parking spaces do we need?

To figure out how many parking spaces you need, simply follow the directions. On question 3 make sure that you count the average attendance of the largest worship service during the previous year. The national average used in planning parking for major malls is 1.75 people per car. As we move further into the twenty-first century more people will come to church one person per car. Studies also show that people tend not to walk more than six hundred feet to a mall door. Church parking lots are much like those at malls. If you plan on building a parking garage, keep in mind that people tend not to use them if it takes more than eight minutes to leave the garage.

When building a new sanctuary or developing a master plan, do not place the sanctuary near the street in front of the parking. Instead, put the parking lot in front of and around the sanctuary or other buildings. Many churches make the mistake of relying on using the parking lot of a nearby business, such as a bank or a supermarket. I know of one church that had virtually no off-street parking of their own, but they had all the parking they needed across the street at a large Sears store. They never dreamed the store would go out of business, but it did, and the church's attendance is rapidly declining.

You can determine the worth of each new parking space by dividing the number of present spaces into the total amount of money you received last year. Every time you reach 80 percent of your capacity, find a way to add 20 percent more parking. There are many ways to do this: (1) The staff and members of the official body who have no trouble walking can covenant together to park on the street in order to leave room for the "yet-to-be-committed." (2) You may want to use the "one, two, three" method of parking used by a growing number of churches. People park bumper to bumper in rows for one-hour parking, two-hour parking, and three-hour parking. Attendants in the lot help people find the right row. One car is always kept on hand for anyone to use in case of an emergency. Provide a parking lot just for visitors.

Action Items for Providing Adequate Parking

1. Add enough parking to provide one space for every two people on the property at the peak hour.
2. Alternately, start a "one, two, three" method of parking in rows.
3. Alternately, obtain a lease on adjacent property and use that property for parking.
4. Alternately, bus your leadership from nearby parking lots.
5. Encourage the staff, members of the official body, and choir members who are in good health to sign a covenant to park off the property. Leaders today need to be seen as servants. The staff should lead the way.

Growth Principle Fourteen:
Decide Whether You Can Build
(Key Questions: 3, 5, 6)

Data Source: Staff Worksheet, questions 103-108

Questions 3, 5: What is our total and potential debt?

Two rules of thumb for debt are helpful. (1) Keep the amount of debt service (monthly mortgage) under 28 percent of the operating budget. (2) Keep the total amount of money owed at or under two times the present operating budget, including the debt service. If you are a rapidly growing church, it is possible to build even when all you have in the bank is eighteen months of debt service payments. You can engage in a bond program. There are three ways to administer bond programs: (1) sell all the bonds, mostly to members of your church; (2) hire someone to sell the bonds, in and out of your church; (3) contract with a bond company to loan you the money and sell the bonds to their clients. Bond programs are preferable to bank loans, not only because they are easier to get, but also because they tie your members closer to the church since the church pays off the bonds they own. More and more churches are paying for new construction as they go so that they do not owe anything after they move in. It is better today to wait to build until you have more money in the bank.

Question 6: When was our last building program?

Fast-growing churches can build every two or three years because of the number of new people who are joining. Unfortunately, some people believe that if they build a facility, people will show up. This has not proved to be true, especially for educational facilities. Something significant has to be happening inside the new facility that addresses a felt need of the community. In the case of a new sanctuary, if the church is providing significant ministries and the area is growing, there is usually a 25 to 30 percent jump in worship attendance the day the new sanctuary is opened.

Action Items for Deciding Whether You Can Build

1. How you fund the project does not matter if the mortgage payment, including debt service, is below 28 percent of your total budget.
2. See appendix 2: Evaluating the Site, Property, and Facilities.

Growth Principle Fifteen:
Seek Nontransfer Growth
(Key Questions: 1, 5, 6, 8-12)

Data Source: Staff Worksheet, questions 109-123; Worship Survey; Chamber of Commerce

Question 1: *How are people joining our church?*

How people are joining is very important, even though membership loss or growth means very little to the health of a church. Most mainline churches will lose 50 percent of their present membership to death over the next twenty-five years. It is better for churches to focus on worship attendance than on membership. The goal is for the people joining by profession of faith (unchurched people) to outnumber the total of people joining by any other method. It is not healthy if the majority of the professions of faith are by confirmation of youth. So the number in the second column is very important. More and more people will have no church background the farther we go into the twenty-first century.

Questions 5, 6: *How far do our members drive?*

The number of miles and minutes people drive to work determines the number of miles and minutes people will drive to church, especially if the church is located along the same route they drive to work.

Question 8: *Who are the unchurched in our area?*

If you do not have a demographic study, call the Chamber of Commerce to get this information. Churches make a major mistake when they ask their members what should be done to reach the community. Church members have very little understanding of the needs of people who have never gone to church. Once a person has been a member of a church for five years, they have a difficult time understanding the needs of the unchurched.

Question 9: *Which group is not being adequately ministered to?*

There is no point in doing something that other churches just like you are doing. Ask yourself whether these churches are just like you and whether what they are doing is of significant quality. Are they targeting the same kind of people you are? Look for the gaps, where your church can do what other churches are not doing and reach people whom other churches are not reaching.

Questions 10, 11: *Is the population of our county or region growing, and are we keeping pace?*

If the population of the area has grown over the past ten years, the church should have grown at or beyond the same rate. However, just because the population is not growing does not mean that the church should not grow. Studies show that communities that experience "turnover" are just as fertile to the church as areas that experience population growth. Turnover growth happens when younger families move into a community as older members of the community move away.

Question 12: *Are the schools in our area full?*

If the schools are full, the church should be full of children. However, often the schools are full of children of different ethnicity than those within the church. This raises a question of morality for the local congregation. Why is this the case?

Action Items for Seeking Nontransfer Growth

1. Provide a demographic study or call the Chamber of Commerce to learn more about the community.
2. Decide if the answer to question 9 is worth pursuing.
3. Strategize about how you can reach more adults by profession of faith.

Growth Principle Sixteen:
Be Friendly Toward Visitors
(Key Questions 1-3, 5, 6, 8-10, 18, 24)

Data Source: Staff Worksheet, questions 121-139; Official Body Worksheet, questions 65-71

Question 1: *How much advertising do we do?*

The larger the church, the more important it is to spend 5 percent of the budget for advertising. The Yellow Pages are the place to begin. Place an ad that stands out and gives a clue about the nature of the church. Avoid the newspaper unless you put your ad in the entertainment or sports section. Radio advertising during drive time is an excellent way for churches of all sizes to target the people they are trying to reach. Direct mail is useful only if you mail to the same people six times during the year. The only exception to this rule is a Christmas card inviting people in the community to the Christmas Eve services. Television is very helpful to large churches with over eight hundred people in worship. Thirty-second television spots six or more times during the week, supplemented by a broadcast of either the worship service or a portion of the worship service on Sunday and at one other time during the week are good. Flyers are the most useless form of advertising. Churches small and large are placing home pages on the World Wide Web. These advertisements include e-mail boxes for the staff, announcements, service times, and links to sites all over the Internet. The cost of advertising in cyberspace can be as little as $500 if you hook up with an association Web server. It is too soon to know if this kind of advertising will add to growth, but many church leaders are betting that they cannot afford to wait while the new reformation is underway.

Questions 2, 3: *How many new families visit each week and how many join?*

These are important indicators of the future growth of a church. The goal is to contact all the people who visit your church (including the people from out of town you may never see again). Studies show that traditional churches must respond within twenty-four hours to those who decide to give you their names, addresses, and phone numbers. This contact needs to be personal and made by a layperson. The layperson can call the visitor on the phone or make what some call a "doorstep visit," taking a gift of some kind and not going inside the door. The key to assimilating new people is introducing them to five to seven new people whom they will consider to be good friends within the first three months of their visiting.

Questions 5, 6: Are we contacting unchurched people?

Studies show that growing churches spend a minimum of twenty hours per week seeking ways to reach and respond to those unchurched people around them and who attend. The staff does research and training, and laypeople do the research and responding. In small churches, usually the pastor responds to visitors. Often, in order to allow the pastor to do this, churches have to reduce the number of meetings they require the pastor to attend. As the church grows, laypeople are trained to do most of the responding to visitors. In nontraditional churches, the major emphasis is on getting new people into small groups.

Question 8: Is every church event a point of entry?

Use every event as an opportunity to invite people to consider the Christian faith and as an opportunity to register the people attending. This applies to everything: musicals, bazaars, fairs, community dinners (consider offering a door prize at the appropriate events so that you can get names, addresses, and phone numbers from the registration forms). Be sure to follow up within the week on those who sign in. Churches tend to make the mistake of not seeing all events as an opportunity to reach into the lives of the unchurched. The best example is weekday childcare. Many churches rent out their facilities to childcare services instead of offering these services themselves. This is a major mistake. Weekday childcare has been one of the best ways to reach into the lives of the unchurched. A church should avoid focusing solely on its membership.

Questions 9, 10: Are we building a mailing list?

Put visitors on the mailing list the first time they register. Send them a letter from the pastor, the newsletter, and a gift and invite them to a small group. The invitation should be extended by the small group leader or by a friend within the small group.

Studies show that friendly, brief visits to first-time visitors within thirty-six hours after they attend will cause 85 percent of them to return the following week. If this home visit is made within seventy-two hours, 60 percent will return. If it is made more than seven days later, 15 percent will return. If the pastor makes this call, each result is cut in half. A phone call by a layperson or the pastor instead of a personal visit cuts results by 80 percent. This immediate response by a layperson is the most important factor in reaching first time visitors. The average person today visits several churches before deciding on a church. This means he or she may not come back for six weeks. By then, the average person decides which church to return to based on the friendliness and helpfulness of the members. If you wait until they return the second time, you lose 85 percent of your visitors.

Concentrate on building your prospect list. You can pick up names from Sunday registration, from contacts members encounter in the routine of business, from real estate transfers, from marriage notices in local newspapers, from families who move into homes next-door to members, from the welcome wagon, from birth notices, and from registration forms for any church programs attended by visitors.

Think of newcomers as "guests" instead of "visitors," and members as "hosts" instead of "greeters." Develop a consistent and workable registration of your visitors at every service, including the Christmas Eve service. The typical registration pad is not the best way to take registration. It does not get most people to register, nor does it get any confidential information. By the time the pad gets to the end of the pew, the rest of the worshipers are doing something else and there is no pressure to sign in. If the pad is passed back to the original position, everyone has the opportunity to see who is on the roll. This is not good because many unchurched boomers and busters want to be anonymous.

Instead of the traditional registration pad, place individual, confidential response cards in the bulletins or on the backs of the pews. Everyone registers at the same time. Encourage everyone to write any prayer requests on the back of the cards and fold them over. Take registration during worship and have the ushers collect the cards right then. Do not do it before the worship service begins. Allow guests in worship to be anonymous if they wish. Do not single them out during worship by asking them to hold up their hands or having them stand or having the members stand. Do not pass the traditional registration pad down the aisle and ask the people to see who on the row is a guest and say hello to them.

Question 18: Do we designate visitor parking?

Designate ten parking spaces for visitors close to the sanctuary door. Paint "Guests" on the curb or car stops or pavement, and put signs up telling visitors that such parking exists. Downtown churches with limited parking need to change "reserved for staff" to "reserved for visitors" on Sunday.

Question 24: Do we provide information packets for visitors?

No one should leave a church without having the opportunity to take information or receive it in the mail. The younger the person, the more important it is that the information be available on a short video instead of print.

Action Items to Capture Visitors

1. Provide 5 percent of your budget for advertising.
2. Set a goal of doubling the first-time visitors if you have fewer than five per week.
3. Respond to visitors within twenty-four hours. Use laypeople.
4. Establish a gift ministry. This means having laypeople deliver a plant, a loaf of bread, or some gift made or grown by the congregation to first-time families within two hours of their visit. To do this you will need color-coded registration cards—one color for members and one for visitors. Take up the cards during worship, sort them during worship, and have the gift, a map, and the gift card ready to be picked up by volunteers after worship and delivered on their way home. Most cities have vendors that provide 8" x 11" "key" maps that break the city into small segments. These are the best kind of maps to give to the people delivering the gifts. Request that the volunteers not go inside: these are "doorstep visits." Using this method, people do not have to go home and then go back out. They can deliver the gift on the way home. Be sure to register attendance on Christmas Eve night.
5. The staff needs to spend twenty hours a week on evangelism.
6. Look at the events you have planned and find ways to involve unchurched people in them.
7. Build up the visitors mailing list by putting first-time visitors on the list.
8. Provide more visitor parking.
9. If you have access to the World Wide Web, use your Web browser to search for the word "worship" and check out how many churches are advertising or conducting communications through the Internet. This will continue to grow as a major source of communicating with the baby busters and millennials over the coming years.

GROWTH PRINCIPLES SEVENTEEN THROUGH TWENTY: MONEY, PLANNING, AND CHANGE

Growth Principle Seventeen:
Don't Be Afraid to Ask for Money
(Key Questions: 1, 4, 6-8, 11, 16, 19, 21, 23, 25, 26, 29, 31, 35-37)

Data Source: Staff Worksheet, questions 140-171; Official Body Worksheet, questions 72-77

Question 1: What are our budget totals?

For the purpose of this section, combine operating and building budgets into one figure. The vast majority of churches have seen their budgets increase over the past ten years even though their worship attendance is declining. Increasing income is never a sign of strength or vitality.

Questions 4, 8: How many persons are involved as workers in the pledge drive?

Traditional churches need to involve at least *one-fourth* of their congregation in the preparation for the actual week or Sunday of gathering the pledges. A minimum of three weeks preparation is necessary so that everyone is aware of the coming pledge drive and has time to think about his or her pledge.

Questions 6, 7: When and how often is our pledge drive?

Traditional churches need to hold a stewardship drive each year if they want to develop solid stewards and budgets. Most churches that rely on a "faith promise" type of stewardship seldom have an annual average giving of $1,000 per person in worship, including children. The best time to conduct a stewardship drive is usually between January and Mother's Day. This means that pledges would not follow a calendar year. Nontraditional churches will do fewer and fewer actual pledge drives. Instead, tithing will be taught in small groups and will probably be required before joining.

Question 11: What is our average pledge?

Are the actual number of pledges increasing? Is the average amount of the pledges increasing each year? Small, growing churches need only 70 percent of their budget covered by the pledges. As the church grows beyond a half-million-dollar budget, the percentage of the budget covered by pledges needs to decrease.

If you have demographics for the area, you need to consider the relation between your budget and the average household income of your members. The goal is for the average family to give 3.5 to 5 percent of its total household income to the church. Average church members give 2.5 percent of their annual household income. In an exceptional church the average giving will reach up to 5 percent of the annual household income. Also, the more people make and the larger the home they live in, the smaller percentage of their income they tend to give.

Question 16: Do we contact new members for a pledge?

Traditional churches need to be intentional about asking new members for pledges within the first month after they join. Develop a method of getting a pledge from each new member of the church. Perhaps start asking them during the membership class. You may want to develop a team of laity who feel comfortable calling those who have not made a pledge. As soon as a person joins, the pastor should send him or her a letter of welcome. This letter should be followed by a letter from the finance chairperson explaining the mission and ministry of the church and its cost. This letter should focus on the mission and ministry, not the financial cost. Enclose a commitment card. If the new members do not return the card within two weeks, do no more at this time until they are welcomed into a small group. Many nontraditional churches (much like synagogues) require a pledge before joining, though many nontraditional independent churches prefer not to have "membership."

Question 19: How are our stewardship campaigns conducted?

It is best not to use the same stewardship campaign more than two or three years in a row. Churches with over three hundred in worship with a large number of people born between 1946 and 1964 need to consider "target stewardship" instead of generic mailings.

Question 21: Do we encourage designated giving?

Designated giving always results in more income and better stewards if a large portion of the congregation is under forty-five years of age. Designated giving will not harm the general budget.

Question 23: How much is our Christmas offering?

The month of December is the best time of the year during which to raise extra income. It is not uncommon for churches with intentional efforts developed over a long period of time to raise as much as an extra month's income. One way to do this is to begin the offering at the beginning of Advent and conclude it Christmas Eve. Send out a letter telling about it and include a printed envelope. Put the same envelope in the bulletin each week. Specifically state where the offering will go.

Question 25: Do we have regular special offerings?

It will help to have two or three special offerings for the budget during the year: at Easter, during summer, and at Christmas.

Question 26: How much does each worshiper give?

The goal is to reach an average annual gift of $1,000 per person, including children.

Question 29: How much is our debt service?

This chart helps you track the percentage of your budget that is devoted to debt and debt service.

Question 31: What are our financial resources?

Most churches have enough money squirreled away in a variety of accounts to turn themselves around. Often these funds have been lying around in these accounts for several years. No one is ever helped to mature in Christ by money gaining interest in the bank. Your task is to put that money to good use. Quit waiting for a rainy day. How much of this money absolutely cannot be used? How much is really designated for a specific item or ministry? It is better to use this money for new ministries or staff that you are certain will meet a need in the community and thus lead to more people hearing the gospel in your church.

Endowments to thrive on, rather than survive on, are essential to the future of many congregations. It is essential to allow people to designate their gift to a variety of long-term options such as (1) giving without any instruction as to how the money can be used; (2) giving with only the interest to be used, designated or undesignated; (3) giving with both the principal and interest to be used; (4) giving money to be used only for building or maintenance; (5) giving money to be used only to establish or sustain a ministry or staff person.

Use the endowment to help you thrive instead of just survive. Use it in a way that secures the future of the church's ministry. It is not a matter of whether it is used for capital improvements or whether it is used for programs. It should be used so that it doesn't become a crutch. Place the endowment ministry under a group concerned with stewardship instead of under the trustees. This way the people will understand that the money can be used for a variety of ministries, not just for buildings. Too many churches have enough money for the buildings to be taken care of long after all the people are all gone.

Questions 35, 36: When do we cut the budget?

Finance committees should go out of their way not to cut the budget. Instead, they should spend a minimum of six months trying to find ways to find the money needed to accomplish new ministries. Most effective ministries do not have to be propped up. They will generate their own income. Finance committees should pray together for ways to lead the congregation into tithing. Usually such changes in giving patterns begin with the leadership changing their habits.

Question 37: When was our last capital fund drive?

In a growing church, capital fund drives can be done every three years.

Action Items for Asking for Money

1. Involve one-third of the church in the leadership of stewardship education before the actual drive.
2. Change your stewardship year from a calendar year to April through March or May through April.
3. Begin an endowment ministry.
4. Set a goal of receiving 3.5 to 5.0 percent of the average member's household income by talking about "stepping up to tithing."

Growth Principle Eighteen:
Lay a Solid Foundation
(Key Questions: 1, 2)

Data Source: Staff Worksheet, questions 172-178; Official Body Worksheet, questions 78-80

Question 1: Do we have a vision?

A vision is realized when the leadership is willing to do whatever is necessary to bring about the vision. Without this vision, churches flounder and decline unless the population around the church is growing fast. Of course, even then the church may decline. Vision is like a rudder and compass on a ship during a major storm. It is the only thing that keeps the church on course.

Question 2: Do we have a clear mission statement?

Perhaps the most important thing a church can do is to understand why it exists and how it is going to live out its ministry. There are three types of statements a church needs to make in order to clarify its reason for existence. The *mission statement* is the basic, bottom-line mission of the church. It is why the church exists. It is what keeps the leaders and various teams in alignment. The more diverse the ministries of the church, the more important the mission statement is. It is seldom longer than a sentence, is easily memorized, and is general in nature. The *vision statement* is the narrowly defined mission of the church. It is slightly longer and much more specific than the mission statement. It steers individuals and teams in the direction a particular body is going and what it hopes to accomplish. A church must be clear about its bottom line in order to develop mission and vision statements. The *value statement* sets the boundaries of opportunity in which individuals and groups within the congregation can live out the above two statements without having to get permission to act. It provides the subtle boundaries that informally sanction or prohibit behavior.

The following are the mission, vision, and value statements for 21st Century Strategies, Inc. I have used our statements as examples only because we are not a church and our statement will not directly influence you as you develop your own statements.

Mission statement:

To provide the networks, environment, and resources to help church leaders transition into the twenty-first century and carry out the Great Commission.

Vision statement:

To equip church leaders for ministry in the twenty-first century by focusing on innovative leaders who realize that ministry-as-usual no longer grows disciples; providing resources, technical support, and opportunities for networking; and training these leaders at large events in all areas of North America and smaller events at or near our facilities.

Value statement:

We value
- teams instead of hierarchies or bureaucracies;
- accountability instead of control;
- servant-oriented people who are willing to take risks;

- networks and alliances instead of denominational affiliations;
- small groups instead of committees;
- mentoring more than confirmation or classes;
- evangelism, social justice, and Christian nurture instead of a narrowly focused faith.

Action Items for Laying a Solid Foundation

I've found the following questions helpful in developing a vision and mission statement:

1. Will our church focus ministry primarily on the needs within our congregation or will we focus as much attention on the needs of the unchurched in the community as we do on ourselves?
2. Can a church be a church without concerning itself about the unchurched around it?
3. Are we going to be a church that depends mostly on the pastor for congregational care and evangelistic outreach or are we going to develop a laity-driven ministry that incorporates both pastoral care and evangelistic outreach?
4. Are we going to be a program-based church that invites people to attend programs led by a professional staff, or are we going to be a small-group-based church that relies less on program and staff and more on the priesthood of the believers and the networking between members and their friends outside the church?
5. Are we going to be basically a Sunday church or are we going to be a seven-day-a-week church, and if so what are our core ministries during the week?
6. Will all of our ministries be conducted on the church property, or will we develop satellite ministries?
7. Are we content with developing worship designed basically for people who are over fifty or who may be under fifty but have never left the church, or are we going to also provide worship designed for people especially in their twenties and thirties who have left the church?
8. What does Acts say about the role of stewardship of money in our lives, and are we living up to the New Testament understanding of tithing?
9. Are we willing to add staff members to the church in order to reach the unchurched, or will we remain staffed as we are?

The ability of your church to reach the unchurched people in your community depends largely on how you decide the above questions.

Growth Principle Nineteen:
Plan Strategically
(Key Questions: 1, 8)

Data Source: Staff Worksheet, question 179; Official Body Worksheet, questions 81-87

Question 1: *Where do we want to go?*

Most forms of strategic planning usually wind up on a shelf gathering dust. To avoid this, strategic planning should not cover more than two or three years. Any plan for longer than that is wasted effort due to the changing nature of our times. Strategic planning is deciding what the church needs to commit to today in order to cause tomorrow to be what the church feels God wants it to be. See any strategic plan as subject to change as the cultural conditions change.

Question 8: *Do we hold people accountable?*

Accountability is essential when a church is trying to navigate through changing times. You will have to try some things you have never tried before. In order to make sure the overall outcome is what you want, you must have accountability. Accountability is not control. Accountability is giving an account of what one has already done. Control is forcing people to get permission before they can act. Accountability is biblical, control is not. The more emphasis you can put on accountability and autonomy among the various ministries of the church, the healthier the church will be. This is especially true if the church stresses spiritual gifts. It does not make sense to encourage people to discover their spiritual gifts and then tell them that they have to get permission to use those gifts.

Action Items for Planning Strategically

1. Develop your mission, vision, and value statements if you have not done so already.
2. Read the following books about strategic planning: Henry Mintzberg, *The Rise and Fall of Strategic Planning*; Peter Schwartz, *The Art of the Long View;* William M. Easum, *The Church Growth Handbook* (see Recommended Reading).
3. Bring in a short-term consultant if you have never developed a master plan before.
4. Don't overplan.

Growth Principle Twenty:
Be Ready to Work Hard and Make Change
(Key Questions: 1-7)

Data Source: Staff Worksheet, questions 180-182; Official Body Worksheet, questions 88-91

Questions 1, 2: *Is our church free from power cliques?*

Every church has power cliques; however, the more powerful the cliques become, the less capable of moving forward the church will be. When one or two people have the ability to sway the direction of a vote, this inhibits the church's growth. The best thing you can do is to quit listening to the power cliques.

Questions 3, 4: *How long have we been members?*

The longer people have been members of the church, the less likely they will understand the hurts and hopes of those who have never been inside a church. If the average leader filling out the Ministry Audit is over forty-five years of age and has been a member for more than five years, it is highly important that you do focus groups with people under forty-five years of age who do not go to church in order to gain insights into who they are and how to reach them.

Questions 5, 6: *How many participated in the audit?*

It is best if a minimum of 25 percent of your leadership fill out the Official Body Worksheet.

Question 7: *Do we make summer schedule changes?*

There is a time not to change (by dropping ministries). The only changes that should be made in the summer are adding ministries. For example, offer an outdoor worship service or plan more youth activities. Avoid combining worship services, changing the times, or dropping Sunday school.

Action Items for Making Change

1. Identify the power cliques and address the problem if they are too powerful.
2. Do not reduce the schedules in the summer; instead, add to the choices.
3. As an indicator of ability to change, see the comments on the worksheet totals for the Staff and Official Body Readiness Worksheets at the end of section 2.
4. As an indicator of how much power is given to cliques, even at the top, see the comments on how to interpret the Staff and Official Body Permission Giving Worksheets at the end of section 2.

WORKSHEET TOTALS

Worship Survey Totals

After conducting the survey in worship for four consecutive Sundays, add the responses from all four weeks together, divide by 4, and record the results below. This total sheet may be found on the bonus software disk under the filename "WRSHPENT.*." The totals can be averaged in the spreadsheet.

1. I was born between

   1983 and 2000 _____

   1965 and 1982 _____

   1946 and 1964 _____

   1925 and 1945 _____

   1900 and 1924 _____

2. My gender is

   Male _____

   Female _____

3. My marital status is

   Married _____

   Single _____

4. The number of people in my car this morning is _____.

5. The number of miles I drive or commute to church is

   Less than one _____

One to three _____

Four to six _____

Seven to ten _____

Ten to fifteen _____

More than fifteen _____

6. My home is N _____   NE _____   E _____   SE _____   S_____   SW _____   W_____   NW_____ of the church.

7. The number of miles I drive or commute to work is _____.

8. The number of minutes I drive or commute to work is _____.

9. On the radio, I prefer to listen to (choose only one)

Country _____

Jazz _____

Classical _____

Christian _____

Hard rock _____

Soft rock _____

Oldies _____

Rap _____

News/Talk _____

National Public Radio _____

10. The magazine I read most is _____.

In the average church, *Reader's Digest* is by far the most widely read book.
Country music is the most popular radio fare.

11. I am a

New visitor _____

Continuing visitor _____

Member _____

12. Our yearly household income is

less than $7,500 _____

$7,500 to $14,999 _____

$15,000 to $24,999 _____

$25,000 to $34,999 _____

$35,000 to $49,999 _____

$50,000 to $74,999 _____
$75,000 to $99,999 _____
$100,000 to $124,999 _____
$125,000 or more _____

Readiness Worksheet Totals

The Readiness Worksheets measure the "Heart Factor" of your church. A response of 1 indicates total agreement with the statement and a response of 10 indicates total disagreement. The lower the score, the more heart the church has for ministry to people, and the better its attitude is regarding what needs to be done in order to reach the unchurched. History has shown that churches with declining attendance and vitality averaging less than 3 on all the questions can reverse their pattern of decline without much difficulty. Declining churches scoring an average between 3 and 4 on all questions can reverse their pattern of decline, but it will be more difficult. Those scoring an average over 4 on all questions have a very difficult time reaching out to the unchurched without a major change in heart and attitude.

The higher the average score on all questions, the more difficult it will be for the church to make a transition, and the slower you should go. If the score is over 4, the congregation needs to spend most of the next year simply focusing on who it is and why it exists. The score on each question also predicts the difficulty the church will have initiating change in a certain area. The higher the score on each question, the more difficult it is to make changes in that area without a change of heart.

The following scores are the averages of the responses from two hundred churches. Every church scores higher on questions 6, 7, and 8 than on the other questions.

Question	Staff	Official Body
1. Nursery	2.02	2.86
2. Turf	2.44	2.95
3. Facilities	1.84	2.48
4. Reach	1.83	1.94
5. Change	2.50	3.34
6. Procedure	4.81	5.08
7. Debt	4.27	5.46
8. Spending	3.21	4.93
9. Worship	2.00	2.42
10. Attention	2.17	2.40
11. Staff	1.62	2.35
12. Trust	1.54	1.96

Examining the following sample readiness charts will give you an idea of how to use the worksheets to get a quick overview of the church's readiness to reach out to the unchurched or pre-Christian community.

Look at the readiness chart for the average church on page 54. It shows the average staff and offical body scores among more than two hundred churches. Notice the following: (1) The scores of the staff are usually lower (more positive toward growth) than those of the official body. When a staff scores higher (more negative toward growth) than the official body, I know some of the staff are resistant to growth. When this occurs, it is good to examine the individual scores to see if there is one staff person skewing the scores with all nines or tens for

READINESS CHART
Average Church Among Two Hundred Churches

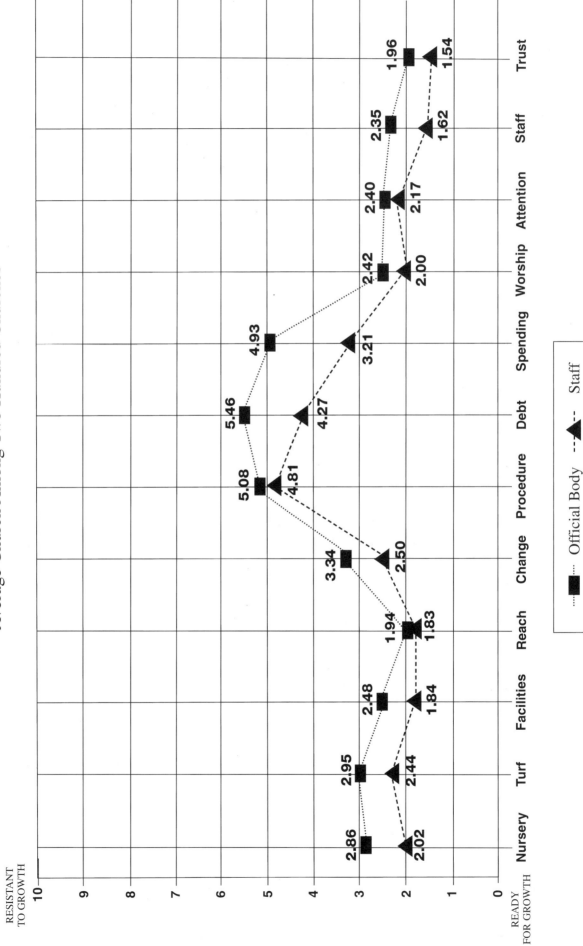

RESISTANT
TO GROWTH

READY
FOR GROWTH

Legend: ····■···· Official Body   - - -▲- - - Staff

Categories: Nursery, Turf, Facilities, Reach, Change, Procedure, Debt, Spending, Worship, Attention, Staff, Trust

Official Body values: Nursery 2.86, Turf 2.95, Facilities 2.48, Reach 1.94, Change 3.34, Procedure 5.08, Debt 5.46, Spending 4.93, Worship 2.42, Attention 2.40, Staff 2.35, Trust 1.96

Staff values: Nursery 2.02, Turf 2.44, Facilities 1.84, Reach 1.83, Change 2.50, Procedure 4.81, Debt 4.27, Spending 3.21, Worship 2.00, Attention 2.17, Staff 1.62, Trust 1.54

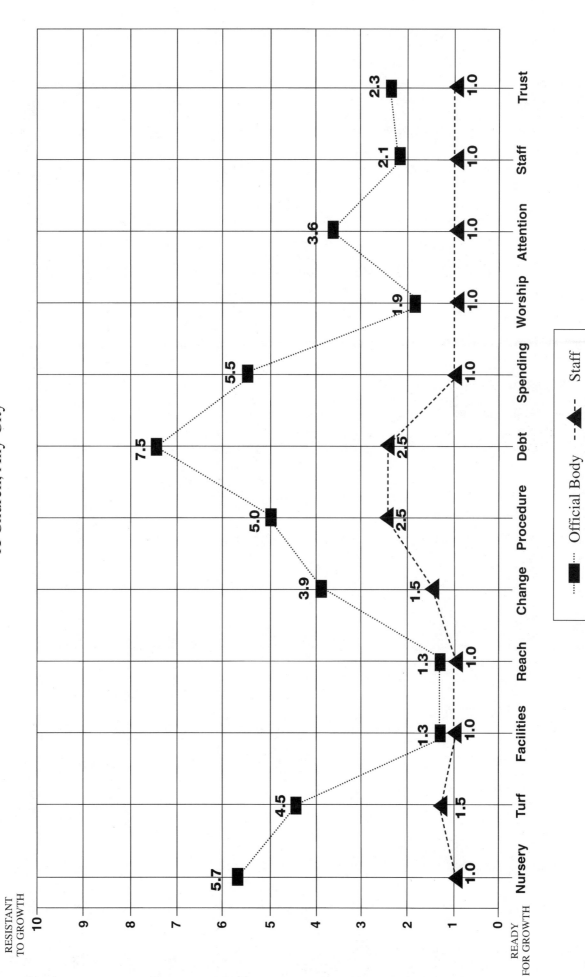

READINESS CHART
X Church, Any City

RESISTANT TO GROWTH

READY FOR GROWTH

■····· Official Body   ◀ - - Staff

Copyright © 1996 by Abingdon Press. Reproduced with permission.

answers. (2) The scores on questions 6, 7, and 8 for both the staff and the official body are normally higher than all the rest, forming a mountain peak on the graph. I expect these to be high and a problem in most churches. When they are low I am surprised and know this is an unusual church. If the scores are significantly higher than average, I know these three areas are going to be very touchy areas for this church. (3) There is usually a close correlation between the answers of the staff and official body. When this is not the case, I know that this is probably a good area to explore with the church leaders to see what I can learn.

The readiness chart for X Church in Any City shows the following: (1) The response to the nursery question tells me that this church does not understand the importance of a nursery. The church leaders probably no longer have any young children at home. The nursery is probably in need of a lot of work. (2) The response to the turf question tells me that it will be hard to move the nursery to a better location. More than likely there are some locked spaces in the kitchen that only a few can use, or a parlor that children can't enter, or some adult classes that can't be moved. (3) The response to the attention question shows that some church leaders see their pastor as their personal chaplain. There are probably a lot of controllers in this church. When the answers to this question are above the 3.0 line, I know that there are serious problems within the staff. (4) The response to the debt question suggests that this church will strongly resist incurring debt. I have found that there is no correlation between the amount of money a church owes and how the church answers this question. Churches with no debt will answer it just as high as churches with very high debt.

Staff Readiness Worksheet Totals

Average the paid staff's responses to the Staff Readiness Worksheet and record them below. This total sheet can be found on the bonus software disk under the filename "STFF2ENT.*." The totals can be averaged in the spreadsheet.

1. The nursery should be extra clean and neat, staffed with paid help, and open every time there is a church function.
   Average of responses: _____

2. Turf issues are harmful to the growth of a church.
   Average of responses: _____

3. I am willing for the facilities to be used even if they get dirty.
   Average of responses: _____

4. Reaching out to new members is just as important as taking care of the present members.
   Average of responses: _____

5. I am comfortable with radical change if it will help my church reach more people for Christ.
   Average of responses: _____

6. I am seldom concerned about procedure.
   Average of responses: _____

7. Paying off the debt is not a major concern to me.
   Average of responses: _____

8. I support the idea of spending some of our church's savings in order to hire more staff or start new programs.
   Average of responses: _____

9. Several worship services are fine with me because I am more interested in meeting the needs of all the people than I am in knowing everyone at church.
   Average of responses: _____

10. I'm not at all offended when my pastor does not give me regular personal attention.
    Average of responses: _____

11. I realize that more staff are needed today than in the past.
    Average of responses: _____

12. I always trust and affirm my pastor's efforts to reach more people for Christ.
    Average of responses: _____

Official Body Readiness Worksheet Totals

Average the official body's responses to the Official Body Readiness Worksheet and record them below. This total sheet can be found on the bonus software disk under the filename "BODY2ENT.*."

1. The nursery should be extra clean and neat, staffed with paid help, and open every time there is a church function.
   Average of responses: _____

2. Turf issues are harmful to the growth of a church.
   Average of responses: _____

3. I am willing for the facilities to be used even if they get dirty.
   Average of responses: _____

4. Reaching out to new members is just as important as taking care of the present members.
   Average of responses: _____

5. I am comfortable with radical change if it will help my church reach more people for Christ.
   Average of responses: _____

6. I am seldom concerned about procedure.
   Average of responses: _____

7. Paying off the debt is not a major concern to me.
   Average of responses: _____

8. I support the idea of spending some of our church's savings in order to hire more staff or start new programs.
   Average of responses: _____

9. Several worship services are fine with me because I am more interested in meeting the needs of all the people than I am in knowing everyone at church.
   Average of responses: _____

10. I'm not at all offended when my pastor does not give me regular personal attention.
    Average of responses: _____

11. I realize that more staff are needed today than in the past.
    Average of responses: _____

12. I always trust and affirm my pastor's efforts to reach more people for Christ.
    Average of responses: _____

Permission Giving Worksheet Totals

The lower the score on each of these questions, the more able the church is to transform into a permission-giving church. If the total for all scores is under 60, you are already a permission-giving church or are ready to become a permission-giving church. If the total for all scores is between 61 and 79, you have some weaknesses in your permission-giving system. Work on the weaknesses and begin the shift gradually. If the total for all scores is over 80, it is too early to begin trying to transform the church. Begin exploring your mission, vision, and value statements.

A permission-giving church empowers people to make on-the-spot decisions and develop new ministries without asking permission from the official body. Each person is held accountable for her or his actions, based on the mission, vision, and value statements of the church. This church is more concerned with sharing the gospel by responding to the felt needs of people in the name of Jesus Christ than with following certain procedures or controlling what people can or can't do.

A permission-giving church is based on trust, collaboration, and networks. It is organized to ensure that old and new ministries take place. The organization focuses on personal and corporate growth instead of institutional growth. This church stresses the spiritual gifts of each person instead of finding people to fill the offices of the church. Chaos is seen as good. New ministries are more important than perpetuating the status quo. Too many churches are organized to prevent anything bad from happening or someone going off on a tangent; as a result of this kind of overcautious organization, they ensure that nothing happens.

Permission-giving churches believe that the role of God's people is to minister to people, in the world, every day of the week, by living out their spiritual gifts instead of running the church by sitting on committees and making decisions about what can or cannot be done. This church seeks unity in the essentials, freedom in the nonessentials, and trust and love in all things. The key elements are empowerment, responsibility, trust, a common mission, freedom, autonomy, decentralization, networks, synergy, and the collaboration of individuals and teams.

In a permission-giving church, the role of laity is to live out their spiritual gifts. People are not asked routinely to serve on committees. Networks encourage autonomous, on-the-spot decision making by individuals and self-organizing, self-governing, self-destructing teams. They encourage ministry to be delivered anytime, anyplace, by anyone, no matter what. They don't give a new ministry to an existing committee to implement. They avoid taking a vote on new ministries whenever possible. They bless diversity more than uniformity and are passionate about providing choices. Representative democracy is unimportant. They have leaders who are secure enough to equip others for ministry and then get out of their way and let them develop their ministry, even if it is not something in which they might participate. Permission-giving churches do need boundaries other than the mission, vision, and value statements. Permission-giving churches develop a flat organizational structure that encourages and facilitates ministry instead of coordinating or managing it. The organization's first goal is to help people grow in their faith, not to "run the church." For more information on how the permission-giving church works, see my book *Sacred Cows Make Gourmet Burgers* (see Recommended Reading).

Staff Permission Giving Worksheet Totals

Average the paid staff's responses to the Staff Permission Giving Worksheet and record them below. This total sheet can be found on the bonus software disk under the filename "STFF3ENT.*."

1. Our church leaders believe that people doing the actual ministry should make the majority of the decisions that affect how they do their ministry.
   Average of responses: _____

2. People at the lowest level of organization in our church should be able to suggest and implement improvements to their own ministry without going through several committees and levels of approval.
   Average of responses: _____

3. Each person in the congregation should be free to live out his or her spiritual gifts in the congregation without getting approval, even if it means starting a new ministry.
   Average of responses: _____

4. The nature of ministry lends itself to a team-based approach rather than to individual effort.
   Average of responses: _____

5. Our leadership is flexible enough to permit restructuring or reorganization in order to facilitate the new mission of the church.
   Average of responses: _____

6. It is possible to organize ministry so that teams can take responsibility for entire ministries.
   Average of responses: _____

7. There is enough complexity in our ministry to allow for initiative and decision making.
   Average of responses: _____

8. Our leadership is comfortable with individuals or teams making autonomous, on-the-spot decisions.
   Average of responses: _____

9. The laity are interested in organizing into teams or small groups or willing to organize into teams or small groups.
   Average of responses: _____

10. Our key leadership is willing to share its power with those who are not in leadership.
    Average of responses: _____

11. Our church has a history of following through on new ideas.
    Average of responses: _____

12. Our key lay leadership is willing to radically change its own roles and behavior.
    Average of responses: _____

13. Our church is secure enough to guarantee a period of relative stability during which permission giving can develop.
    Average of responses: _____

14. We have adequate resources to support and train our people.
    Average of responses: _____

15. Our staff and key lay leadership understands that becoming a permission-giving church is a lengthy, time-consuming, and labor-intensive process that may take five years and is willing to make the investment in time.
    Average of responses: _____

16. Our church has a network that could provide information to any layperson anytime.
    Average of responses: _____

17. Our laypeople have the skills needed to take greater responsibility for the ministries of the church.
    Average of responses: _____

18. Our senior pastor is willing to invest in training the team leaders.
    Average of responses: _____

19. Our finance and trustee committees should exist to serve the needs of the those trying to implement ministry.
    Average of responses: _____

20. Our leaders are more concerned with discovering ways to reach the unchurched than with how those ministries are discovered or implemented.
    Average of responses: _____

Official Body Permission Giving Worksheet Totals

Average the official body's responses to the Official Body Permission Giving Worksheet and record them below. This total sheet can be found on the bonus software disk under the filename "BODY3ENT.*." The totals can be averaged in the spreadsheet.

1. Our church leaders believe that people doing the actual ministry should make the majority of the decisions that affect how they do their ministry.
   Average of responses: _____

2. People at the lowest level of organization in our church should be able to suggest and implement improvements to their own ministry without going through several committees and levels of approval.
   Average of responses: _____

3. Each person in the congregation should be free to live out his or her spiritual gifts in the congregation without getting approval, even if it means starting a new ministry.
   Average of responses: _____

4. The nature of ministry lends itself to a team-based approach rather than to individual effort.
   Average of responses: _____

5. Our leadership is flexible enough to permit restructuring or reorganization in order to facilitate the new mission of the church.
   Average of responses: _____

6. It is possible to organize ministry so that teams can take responsibility for entire ministries.
   Average of responses: _____

7. There is enough complexity in our ministry to allow for initiative and decision making.
   Average of responses: _____

8. Our leadership is comfortable with individuals or teams making autonomous, on-the-spot decisions.
   Average of responses: _____

9. The laity are interested in organizing into teams or small groups or willing to organize into teams or small groups.
   Average of responses: _____

10. Our key leadership is willing to share its power with those who are not in leadership.
    Average of responses: _____

11. Our church has a history of following through on new ideas.
    Average of responses: _____

12. Our key lay leadership is willing to radically change its own roles and behavior.
    Average of responses: _____

13. Our church is secure enough to guarantee a period of relative stability during which permission giving can develop.
    Average of responses: _____

14. We have adequate resources to support and train our people.
    Average of responses: _____

15. Our staff and key lay leadership understands that becoming a permission-giving church is a lengthy, time-consuming, and labor-intensive process that may take five years and is willing to make the investment in time.
    Average of responses: _____

16. Our church has a network that could provide information to any layperson anytime.
    Average of responses: _____

17. Our laypeople have the skills needed to take greater responsibility for the ministries of the church.
    Average of responses: _____

18. Our senior pastor is willing to invest in training the team leaders.
    Average of responses: _____

19. Our finance and trustee committees should exist to serve the needs of those trying to implement ministry.
    Average of responses: _____

20. Our leaders are more concerned with discovering ways to reach the unchurched than with how those ministries are discovered or implemented.
    Average of responses: _____

Section Three

WORKSHEETS

This section contains the worksheets that you will use to prepare the audit. The Complete Ministry Audit is the last document in section 3. Before you complete the actual audit worksheet, you are advised to (a) photocopy the audit for use in subsequent years, (b) make use of the ASCII text file ("AUDIT.TXT") found on the bonus software disk in your favorite word processor, or (c) purchase another copy of this book from your Christian bookstore.

Several of the worksheets are supplied on the bonus software disk in spreadsheet form for your use if you have access to a personal computer that runs Windows versions of Excell or Lotus 1-2-3 or if you use a spreadsheet program that imports these files. The filenames are in parentheses below. For the Staff Worksheet, only portions of the worksheet are appropriate in spreadsheet form, and thus there is no data entry version. The other worksheets, however, are set up as data entry spreadsheets. Those files with names ending in "ENT" are for data entry. See the appendix for more instructions on how to make the bonus software disk work for you.
The worksheets are as follows:

Worship Survey ("WORSHIP.*" and "WRSHPENT.*")

Staff Worksheet ("STAFF1.*" and "STFF1ENT.*")

Staff Readiness Worksheet ("STAFF2.*" and "STFF2ENT.*")

Staff Permission Giving Worksheet ("STAFF3.*" and "STFF3ENT.*")

Official Body Worksheet ("BODY1.*" and "BODY1ENT.*")

Official Body Readiness Worksheet ("BODY2.*" and "BODY2ENT.*")

Official Body Permission Giving Worksheet ("BODY3.*" and "BODY3ENT.*")

The Complete Ministry Audit ("AUDIT.TXT")

You may make a copy of the blank Ministry Audit so that you can use it again on an annual basis, or you may order fresh copies of this book through your favorite bookstore or by calling 1-800-672-1789.

If you would like the author of this book, William Easum, to perform an analysis of your completed audit—for a fee—you may call the author at 512-749-5364.

WORSHIP SURVEY

For four consecutive Sundays we will be conducting a survey during our worship service. We will be using the information in our Ministry Audit.

If you were born before 1983, please take a few minutes to fill out this survey *each Sunday*, even if you filled one out the preceding week.

* * * *

1. I was born between

    1965 and 1982 _____

    1946 and 1964 _____

    1925 and 1945 _____

    1900 and 1924 _____

2. My gender is

    Male _____

    Female _____

3. My marital status is

    Married _____

    Single _____

4. The number of people in my car this morning is _____.

5. The number of miles I drive or commute to church is

    Less than one _____

    One to three _____

    Four to six _____

Seven to ten _____

Ten to fifteen _____

More than fifteen _____

6. My home is N _____ NE _____ E _____ SE _____ S _____ SW _____

   W _____ NW _____ of the church.

7. The number of miles I drive or commute to work is _____.

8. The number of minutes I drive or commute to work is _____.

9. On the radio, I prefer to listen to

   Country _____

   Jazz _____

   Classical _____

   Christian _____

   Hard rock _____

   Soft rock _____

   Oldies _____

   Rap _____

   News/Talk _____

   National Public Radio _____

10. The magazine I read most is _____.

11. I am a

    New visitor _____

    Continuing visitor _____

    Member _____

12. Our yearly household income is

    less than $7,500 _____

    $7,500 to $14,999 _____

    $15,000 to $24,999 _____

    $25,000 to $34,999 _____

    $35,000 to $49,999 _____

    $50,000 to $74,999 _____

    $75,000 to $99,999 _____

    $100,000 to $124,999 _____

    $125,000 or more _____

STAFF WORKSHEET

CHURCH: _____

DATE: _____

In order to answer questions 1, 98, 112, 113, and 114, you will refer to the completed Worship Surveys.

1. What is the age, sex, and marital status of adult worshipers? (Gather this information from the Worship Survey, question 1.)

M/M = Male/Married, M/S = Male/Single, F/M = Female/Married, F/S = Female/Single

BIRTH YEARS

1965–1982	1946–1964	1925–1945	1900–1924
no.: _____	no.: _____	no.: _____	no.: _____
%: _____	%: _____	%: _____	%: _____
M/M_____	M/M_____	M/M_____	M/M_____
M/S _____	M/S _____	M/S _____	M/S _____
F/M _____	F/M _____	F/M _____	F/M _____
F/S _____	F/S _____	F/S _____	F/S _____

Male _____%   Married _____%

Female _____%   Single _____%

How does this compare to the statistics for our area? (Contact the Chamber of Commerce for this information if a percept demographics profile was not ordered.)

1965–1982	1946–1964	1925–1945	1900–1924
_____%	_____%	_____%	_____%

2. What are our people programs, including specialized ministries?

_____

_____

_____

3. Has there been any major controversy or division in the past five years?

_____

_____

4. What is our decision-making process?

_____

_____

5. What percentage of the total budget is devoted to programs? (Do not count salaries as program money.)

_____

Is it 10 percent? _____

6. Who gives or withholds permission for new ideas or ministries in our church?

_____

_____

7. What is our church known for on the community grapevine?

_____

_____

8. Describe our church's organizational structure.

_____

_____

9. Does our church offer a balanced ministry?
   List the various programs under the following headings:
   Love (Nurture) _____

_____

   Justice (Social Action) _____

_____

   Mercy (Evangelism) _____

_____

10. Does our church offer more than one Sunday morning worship service? _____
    At what times?   _____   _____   _____

11. If our church offers more than one worship service, does the same pastor preach each service, or is there a choice? _____

12. Does our church have a preschool? _____

    How many attend? _____

13. Does our church have a grade school? _____

    How many attend? _____

14. Does our church have a parent's day out program? _____

15. Does our church have a day care? _____

    How many attend? _____

16. Do we start a new Sunday school class every three to six months? _____

17. Number of adult Sunday school classes: _____

    How many attend? _____

18. Number of singles' Sunday school classes: _____

    How many attend? _____

19. Number of youth Sunday school classes: _____

    How many attend? _____

20. Number of children's Sunday school classes: _____

    How many attend? _____

21. When was the newest adult Sunday school class started? _____

22. List Sunday evening programs and approximate attendance: _____

    _____

    _____

23. List midweek programs and approximate attendance: _____

    _____

    _____

24. List Bible studies and approximate attendance: _____

    _____

    _____

25. List athletic programs: _____

    _____

    _____

26. List other programs: _____

_____

_____

27. What is our nominating process? _____

_____

28. Do we encourage and use spiritual gift inventories? _____

29. List the membership figures for the past ten years, beginning with the most recent year.

Year	Membership

30. List our losses in membership for the past ten years, beginning with the most recent year.

Year	Death	Withdrawal	Transfer (to same denom.)	Transfer (to other denom.)	Total

31. Our dropout rate for the past year was _____. (Divide last year's total number of losses into the total membership at the end of the year.)

Ten-year average is _____.

32. Do we concentrate on assimilating new members within their first three months? _____

33. Is a staff person or a volunteer responsible for assimilation of new members? _____

34. Does our church have enough small groups? _____
    a. Divide average worship attendance by 10: _____; this is the ideal number of small groups for our church.
    b. Count the number of small groups with fifteen or less in attendance (include Sunday school classes): _____
    c. Subtract line a from line b to determine the number over or under what is needed: _____

35. List the number of each of the following small groups
    a. Recovery _____
    b. Support _____
    c. Learning _____
    d. Mission or discipling _____
    e. Institutional (required denominational) _____
    f. Sunday school _____

36. How many inactive families do we have? _____

37. What percent of the congregation is inactive? _____

38. Do we have an active program to reinstate our inactives? _____

39. Have we cleaned our rolls within the past three years? _____

40. Describe our assimilation program.

_____
_____
_____
_____
_____
_____
_____
_____

41. List the amount of money given to all causes outside our congregation for the past ten years. Include all denominational requirements (for example, apportionments). List the most recent year first.

Year	Amount Given

42. List our programs that are social or political in nature.

_____

_____

_____

43. On how many Sundays during the year is there a sermon from our senior pastor? _____

44. On how many Sundays during the year does the service contain a sermon? _____

45. On how many Sundays during the year is there a sermon from our associate pastor? _____

46. Size of our present adult and youth choirs and services at which they sing:

Choir	Service	Present Size	Ideal Size*

*To determine the ideal size for each choir, divide the attendance at the service at which the choir sings by 10.

47. What is the percentage of worship attendance to membership? _____

48. Do we have an attendance tracking system? _____

   Do we use it? _____

49. Analysis of our worship growth pattern for the past ten years, starting with the current year:

Year	Average Attendance	Percent Increase (+) or Decrease (−)

Worship has increased/decreased _____ percent in the past ten years.

To determine the percentage of growth or decline each year, take, for example, the amount of difference between year 1 and year 2 and divide it by year 1.

50. How much money do we budget for worship? (Include only program money spent on congregation; exclude salaries.) _____

    Is this 25 percent of the program budget? _____

51. How many morning worship services do we offer? _____

    At what times? _____

52. Average attendance at each: _____   _____   _____

53. When was the newest service started? _____

54. Does each service have a regular choir? _____

55. Is there a youth choir that sings regularly? _____

56. On how many Sundays per year does our major adult choir sing? _____

57. How many musicals, cantatas, or dramas does our major choir present each year? _____

58. Does our major adult choir take time off during the year? _____

59. How many children's choirs does our church have? _____
    How often do they sing? _____

60. How many Christmas Eve services does our church have? _____
    Describe each.

    _____

    _____

    _____

    _____

61. Do we offer worship on a day other than Sunday? _____

62. List all senior pastors, with dates of service, for the past twenty years.

Pastor	Dates of Service
	19_____–19_____
	19_____–19_____
	19_____–19_____
	19_____–19_____
	19_____–19_____
	19_____–19_____
	19_____–19_____
	19_____–19_____
	19_____–19_____
	19_____–19_____
	19_____–19_____
	19_____–19_____
	19_____–19_____
	19_____–19_____
	19_____–19_____

63. Tenure of present pastor (or pastors): _____

64. How much vacation do our pastors and staff receive?

    _____

    _____

65. List all current paid staff, giving name, job title, salary, length of service, and whether they are full-time or part-time. Use a separate sheet of paper if necessary. (Add up program staff and support staff separately; see growth principle 10, question 2.)

    _____

    _____

_____
_____
_____
_____
_____
_____
_____
_____
_____
_____
_____
_____
_____
_____
_____
_____
_____
_____
_____
_____
_____
_____

66. Has staff kept pace with growth? _____

67. Are we staffed for decline, maintenance, or growth (based on the answer to question 65)? _____

68. What is the role of our associate pastor? (Apprentice? Professional? Retired?) _____

69. Does our paid staff have opportunities to develop both relational and functional skills? _____

70. Does our paid staff hold weekly staff meetings? _____

71. Does each paid staff member have an opportunity to have input into the staff agenda? _____

72. Are new ideas from the paid staff welcome at the staff meetings? _____

73. Does the paid staff have yearly retreats? _____

74. Does the paid staff gather on Sunday mornings to coordinate the day's events, including worship? _____

75. What percent of our budget do our salaries represent? _____

For churches with less than two hundred in worship, adequate salaries should equal 60 percent of the total budget. For churches with two hundred or more in worship, adequate salaries should equal 40 percent of the total budget.

76. Does our pastor set aside a certain time each week when individual paid staff members can make appointments to consult with him or her? _____

77. Does the pastor share his or her vision for the congregation at the staff meetings? _____

78. Has our staff had formal training in time management? _____

79. Describe the teaching ministries of our church and the role our staff plays in these ministries.

    _____

    _____

    _____

    _____

    _____

80. Use the following chart to determine the actual size of our church in relation to other Protestant churches in the United States.

Average Worship Attendance	Larger Than _____ Percent of Churches
1-49	40.5
50-74	57.5
75-99	69.1
100-149	81.6
150-199	88.6
200-349	96.3
350-499	98.4
500-749	99.3
750-999	99.6
1000+	99.7

    Based on these figures, our church is larger than _____ percent of all Protestant churches. (These figures may vary a few percentage points from denomination to denomination.)

81. Is our leadership's perception of our church's size the same as the reality of our church's size? _____

82. What is our greatest challenge in developing lay leaders? (Recruitment? Equipping? Identifying? Deployment?) _____

83. In the past has our church missed any "windows of opportunity"? _____

84. Do we need more worship space? _____

    (Do not estimate or rely on an architect's estimate. Measure your sanctuary's capacity by actually counting the number of people that can comfortably fit on a pew and multiplying this number by the number of pews in the sanctuary. Alternately, you can measure the total length of all the pews in the sanctuary and divide by 22 inches.)

   a. Sanctuary capacity: _____

   b. Eighty percent of capacity: _____

   c. Average attendance at largest service: _____
      (If c is larger than b, your church needs more worship space.)

85. Is our worship capacity more than 50 percent larger than our Sunday school capacity? (Compare line 84a, above, with line 88a, below.) _____

86. Do we need more choir space? _____

   a. Choir space capacity: _____

   b. Eighty percent of capacity: _____

   c. Average attendance in the largest choir: _____
      (If line c is larger than line b, the answer to question 86 is yes.)

87. Do we need more nursery space? _____

   a. Nursery capacity: _____

   b. Eighty percent of capacity: _____

   c. Average attendance during the largest service: _____
      (If line c is larger than line b, the answer to question 87 is yes.)

Number of nursery personnel during the largest service: _____

   Is the nursery available during all events? _____

   Are infants and toddlers separated? _____

   Are there any written nursery policies that are given to the parents? _____

88. Do we need more education space? _____
   Allow thirty square feet per person for kindergarten and under; twenty square feet per person for first grade and up. Draw a floor plan for each level of each building and show the capacity of each room and the average attendance of each class. From this figure calculate the education capacity.

   a. Education capacity: _____

   b. Eighty percent of capacity: _____

   c. Average attendance: _____
      (If line c is larger than line b, the answer to question 88 is yes.)

89. Is the attendance at each one of our Sunday school classes under 80 percent of the capacity for its space?

   _____

90. Which classes are filled to over 80 percent capacity? _____

   Do we need to rearrange any of these classes? _____

91. Number of classrooms available: _____

   Number of classrooms presently used: _____

92. Do we offer satellite ministries off of our property? _____

93. List the total Sunday school average attendance and percent of growth for the past ten years, beginning with the current year.

Year	Average Attendance	Percent Increase (+) or Decrease (–)

Sunday school attendance has increased/decreased _____ percent over the past ten years.

94. Do we have more than one session of Sunday school? _____
    If so, please list times and attendance of each:

    _____

    _____

    _____

95. According to the 80 percent rule, does our church need to add space? _____
    If so, where?

    _____

    _____

    _____

96. Does our church own enough land? _____

    If our church owns less than eight acres, is there adjacent property for sale? _____

    We own: _____

    We need: _____

97. What is the average attendance at our largest service? (If Sunday school and worship occur at the same hour and the total of these two is larger than the average attendance at any one other worship service, then count the total of Sunday school and worship attendance and place the number here.) _____

98. Average number of people per car (from Worship Survey, question 4): _____

99. Paved off-street parking spaces available (please count): _____

100. Eighty percent of parking capacity (multiply line 99 by 0.80): _____

101. Number of spaces needed to accommodate attendance (divide line 97 by line 98): _____

102. How many spaces do we need to add? _____
(Subtract line 6 from line 7. If line 6 is larger than line 7, no more spaces are needed. Remember: This is an immediate need and does not consider future growth.)

103. Approximately what would be the yearly debt service on the new facility we need to build? _____

104. What percent of our budget would this be? _____

105. a. Our total indebtedness is _____.

b. Our present debt service represents _____ percent of our total budget. (See growth principle 17, question 29.)

106. What percentage of our total budget would our debt service be if we were to add a new facility? (Add line 103 to line 105.) _____

107. When was our last building program? _____

108. What did we build? _____

109. Use the table below to analyze the new membership over the past ten years. How many new members joined by profession of faith? How many transferred from a church of another denomination? How many transferred from a church of the same denomination? (List the current year first.)

Year	Prof. of Faith	Other Denom.	Same Denom.	Total
TOTALS:				

110. Does column 1 outnumber columns 2 and 3? _____

111. Do we intentionally reach out to the unchurched? _____

112. What is the average number of miles our members drive to work? (See Worship Survey, question 7.)

    _____

113. What is the average number of minutes our members drive to work? (See Worship Survey, question 8.)

    _____

114. What is the average number of miles our members drive to church? (See Worship Survey, question 5.)

    _____

(If the answer to question 112 is larger than the answer to question 114, concentrate on meeting the needs of the people who drive longer distances to work.)

Answers to questions 115, 116, 118 and 120 can be obtained through the Chamber of Commerce or through Percept.

115. How many people live within a ten-mile radius of the church? _____
    Sixty percent of these are unchurched prospects.

116. Who are these unchurched people?
    Singles, never married _____
    Single-parent families _____
    Singles, divorced _____
    Young families _____
    Older families _____
    Middle-aged families _____
    Senior citizens _____
    Black _____
    Brown _____
    White _____
    Yellow _____
    Other _____

117. Which group is not being adequately ministered to in our area? (Call the churches in your area and inquire what programs they offer.)

    _____

    _____

118. Has the population of our county increased or decreased over the past ten years? _____
    By how much? _____

119. Has our church kept pace with the population increase/decrease of our county? _____

120. Are the schools full in our area? _____

121. How many dollars and what percent of our budget do we devote to the following forms of advertising?
    Yellow Pages $_____

Newspaper	$_____
Flyers	$_____
Radio	$_____
Television	$_____
Direct Mail	$_____
Other	$_____
TOTAL	$_____
PERCENT OF BUDGET	_____%

Does the total amount represent 5 percent of our budget? _____

122. How many new families visit each week? _____

Do we contact them within forty-eight hours? _____

123. What percent of these families join our church? _____

(Multiply line 122 by 52 and divide that number into the number of new families that join in a year.)

124. What brought these families to our church?

Friends and relatives _____

Driving by _____

Newspaper _____

Yellow Pages _____

Preschool _____

Singles' groups _____

Television _____

Banner _____

Direct mail _____

Other _____

125. How many contacts with unchurched people are made each week? _____

126. Does someone on our staff work on behalf of the unchurched twenty hours each week? _____

127. Do we make it clear in worship that we expect visitors each Sunday? _____

Does our bulletin reflect this? _____

128. How many visitors are added to our mailing list each week? _____

129. Do we put visitors on the mailing list the first time they visit? _____

130. Do we promote Christmas Eve services by having adequate space and advertising? _____

131. Do we provide different colored registration cards for visitors? _____

132. Do we have an evangelism team? _____

133. What group of people or segment of the population can we reach that no one else is ministering to?

_____

134. Do we designate 10 percent of our parking spaces for visitors? _____

135. Do our members wear name tags? _____

136. Does our church have a new members class? _____

137. Do we provide tours of the facilities? _____

138. Do we provide information packets for visitors? _____

139. Do we have a booth or a designated area for information? _____

    If so, is it well marked? _____

140. List budget totals for the past ten years, including operational and debt service, beginning with the most recent year.

Year	Budget Total

141. Is at least one-fourth of our worshiping congregation involved in the preparation for our pledge drives?

_____

142. Do we have a pledge drive every year for the budget? _____

143. At what time of the year is the pledge drive? _____

144. Do we have at least three weeks of education prior to taking pledges? _____

145. Does our pledge card ask only for money? _____

146. List the number and average of pledges for the past five years, beginning with the most recent year.

Year	# Pledges	Avg. Amount	Total Pledges	Budget	% of Budget
TOTALS:					

147. Do our pledges underwrite no more than 70 to 90 percent of our budget? _____

148. Has the amount and the number of pledges increased or decreased each year? _____

149. Based on our record, what kind of income can we expect next year if we change nothing?

Pledges from current members	$_____
Pledges from new members*	$_____
Loose plate offerings	$_____
Regular non-pledgers	$_____
Building usage fees	$_____
Foundation	$_____
Special offerings	$_____
Sunday school offerings	$_____
Interest	$_____
Memorials	$_____
Other	$_____
TOTAL	$_____

*If you discount your total pledges from current members to reflect your historical pledge loss, then count your anticipated pledges from new members after you have divided them by 2. If you do not discount the total pledges from current members, then do not count anticipated pledges from new members.

150. Do we select our stewardship leaders based on their giving patterns and willingness to give of themselves?

_____

151. Do we contact new members for pledges? _____

152. Do we keep detailed records of giving and pledge patterns and analyze them regularly? _____

153. Is our pledge program centered around tithing? _____

154. How are our stewardship campaigns conducted?

_____

_____

155. Describe our past three stewardship programs.

_____

_____

_____

156. Do we encourage designated giving and discourage a unified budget? _____

157. Does our pledge card offer us choices? _____

158. Does our Christmas offering equal at least one-half of one month's income? _____

159. Do we personalize our pledge program? _____

160. Do we have regular special offerings for items within the budget? _____

161. Complete the following for the past ten years beginning with the most recent year.

Year	Average Worship Attendance	Percent of Budget to Average Worship Attendance*	Percent of Budgeted Income to Average Worship Attendance**

*Divide worship total into budget total for each year.
**Divide worship total into budgeted income total for each year. Budgeted income is the actual amount the church received—not what it budgeted.

162. Does our total budget income (operating and building) equal or exceed $1,000 for every person in worship on an average Sunday? (See above chart.) _____

163. Does one-third of our church's income come from no more than one-fourth of our pledges? _____

164. Complete the following chart on indebtedness for the past ten years, beginning with the most recent year.

Year	Total Indebtedness	Indebtedness: Percent of Budget*	Budgeted Debt Service (Mortgage)	Debt Service:** Percent of Budget

*Divide budget total into indebtedness total for each year.
**Divide budget total into budgeted debt service total for each year.

165. Is our debt service under 25 percent of our total operating budget? (See above chart.) _____

166. List of financial resources:

Endowments	$_____
Wills	$_____
Capital fund pledges	$_____
Cash reserves	$_____
Foundation	$_____
Stocks and bonds	$_____
Other	$_____
TOTAL	$_____

167. Is there a plan to use this money? _____

168. Before we retire a mortgage do we designate a new ministry to use the same amount of money we have been using to pay the mortgage? _____

169. Do we allow the use of plaques that recognize those who have given generously? _____

170. When was our last capital funds drive? _____

171. Does our pastor know what each member gives? _____

172. Does our church have a mission statement that is clear, concise, and open-ended? _____

173. Does our church have a logo other than our denominational logo? _____

174. Does our church have an anthem? _____

175. If we do have a logo and an anthem, are they used consistently? _____

176. Do we have a regularly updated five- or ten-year plan? _____

177. Do we have a master plan for the use of land and facilities? _____

178. When was the last time we did strategic planning? _____

179. List present officially adopted objectives or goals of the church.

_____

_____

_____

180. How many people received the Official Body Worksheet? _____

181. How many people completed the Official Body Worksheet? _____

182. Do we make any changes in our schedule in the summer? _____

If so, what are they?

_____

_____

_____

STAFF READINESS WORKSHEET

This worksheet is to be completed by *each* staff member separately. Answers should then be averaged on the total sheet in the Ministry Audit.

CHURCH: _____

DATE: _____

Decide how you *feel* about the following statements, rating your agreement or disagreement with each statement on a scale of one to ten. One means that you totally agree with the statement; ten means that you totally disagree with the statement.

1. The nursery should be extra clean and neat, staffed with paid help, and open every time there is a church function.

   1   2   3   4   5   6   7   8   9   10

2. Turf issues are harmful to the growth of a church.

   1   2   3   4   5   6   7   8   9   10

3. I am willing for the facilities to be used even if they get dirty.

   1   2   3   4   5   6   7   8   9   10

4. Reaching out to new members is just as important as taking care of the present members.

   1   2   3   4   5   6   7   8   9   10

5. I am comfortable with radical change if it will help my church reach more people for Christ.

   1   2   3   4   5   6   7   8   9   10

6. I am seldom concerned about procedure.

   1   2   3   4   5   6   7   8   9   10

7. Paying off the debt is not a major concern to me.

       1   *2*   *3*   *4*   *5*   *6*   *7*   *8*   *9*   *10*

8. I support the idea of spending some of our church's savings in order to hire more staff or start new programs.

       1   *2*   *3*   *4*   *5*   *6*   *7*   *8*   *9*   *10*

9. Several worship services are fine with me because I am more interested in meeting the needs of all the people than I am in knowing everyone at church.

       1   *2*   *3*   *4*   *5*   *6*   *7*   *8*   *9*   *10*

10. I'm not at all offended when my pastor does not give me regular personal attention.

       1   *2*   *3*   *4*   *5*   *6*   *7*   *8*   *9*   *10*

11. I realize that more staff are needed today than in the past.

       1   *2*   *3*   *4*   *5*   *6*   *7*   *8*   *9*   *10*

12. I always trust and affirm my pastor's efforts to reach more people for Christ.

       1   *2*   *3*   *4*   *5*   *6*   *7*   *8*   *9*   *10*

STAFF PERMISSION GIVING WORKSHEET

This worksheet is to be completed by *each* staff member separately. Answers should then be averaged on the total sheet in the Ministry Audit.

CHURCH: _____

DATE: _____

Decide how you *feel* about the following statements, rating your agreement or disagreement with each statement on a scale of one to ten. One means that you totally agree with the statement; ten means that you totally disagree with the statement.

1. Our church leaders believe that people doing the actual ministry should make the majority of the decisions that affect how they do their ministry.

   1   2   3   4   5   6   7   8   9   10

2. People at the lowest level of organization in our church should be able to suggest and implement improvements to their own ministry without going through several committees and levels of approval.

   1   2   3   4   5   6   7   8   9   10

3. Each person in the congregation should be free to live out his or her spiritual gifts in the congregation without getting approval, even if it means starting a new ministry.

   1   2   3   4   5   6   7   8   9   10

4. The nature of ministry lends itself to a team-based approach rather than to individual effort.

   1   2   3   4   5   6   7   8   9   10

5. Our leadership is flexible enough to permit restructuring or reorganization in order to facilitate the new mission of the church.

   1   2   3   4   5   6   7   8   9   10

6. It is possible to organize ministry so that teams can take responsibility for entire ministries.

   1   2   3   4   5   6   7   8   9   10

7. There is enough complexity in our ministry to allow for initiative and decision making.

   1   2   3   4   5   6   7   8   9   10

8. Our leadership is comfortable with individuals or teams making autonomous, on-the-spot decisions.

   1   2   3   4   5   6   7   8   9   10

9. The laity are interested in organizing into teams or small groups or willing to organize into teams or small groups.

   1   2   3   4   5   6   7   8   9   10

10. Our key leadership is willing to share its power with those who are not in leadership.

    1   2   3   4   5   6   7   8   9   10

11. Our church has a history of following through on new ideas.

    1   2   3   4   5   6   7   8   9   10

12. Our key lay leadership is willing to radically change its own roles and behavior.

    1   2   3   4   5   6   7   8   9   10

13. Our church is secure enough to guarantee a period of relative stability during which permission giving can develop.

    1   2   3   4   5   6   7   8   9   10

14. We have adequate resources to support and train our people.

    1   2   3   4   5   6   7   8   9   10

15. Our staff and key lay leadership understand that becoming a permission-giving church is a lengthy, time-consuming, and labor-intensive process that may take five years and is willing to make the investment in time.

    1   2   3   4   5   6   7   8   9   10

16. Our church has a network that could provide information to any layperson anytime.

    1   2   3   4   5   6   7   8   9   10

17. Our laypeople have the skills needed to take greater responsibility for the ministries of the church.

    1   2   3   4   5   6   7   8   9   10

18. Our senior pastor is willing to invest in training the team leaders.

    1   2   3   4   5   6   7   8   9   10

19. Our finance and trustee committees should exist to serve the needs of those trying to implement ministry.

    1   2   3   4   5   6   7   8   9   10

20. Our leaders are more concerned with discovering ways to reach the unchurched than with how those ministries are discovered or implemented.

    1   2   3   4   5   6   7   8   9   10

OFFICIAL BODY WORKSHEET

This questionnaire is to be completed by *each* member of the church's official administrative body—that is, the church board, the administrative board, the elders, the session, or however you designate the body of church officials.

CHURCH: _____

DATE: _____

Please respond to each of the following questions using a scale of one to ten, one meaning an unqualified yes and ten meaning an unqualified no. (Some questions ask for a written response rather than a number.) Your answers will be averaged and inserted into the Ministry Audit.

1. Does our pastor understand the everyday world of our members?
   1   2   3   4   5   6   7   8   9   10

2. Does our church deal openly with controversy?
   1   2   3   4   5   6   7   8   9   10

3. Do our official administrative body and committee members understand the difference between a working board and an information board?
   1   2   3   4   5   6   7   8   9   10

4. If our official administrative body consists of more than twenty-five people do we have an official executive committee to do the basic work?
   1   2   3   4   5   6   7   8   9   10

5. Can ministry decisions be made quickly without a lot of red tape?
   1   2   3   4   5   6   7   8   9   10

6. Can new members be added to committees and the official administrative body without major delay?
   1   2   3   4   5   6   7   8   9   10

7. Do we make most of our ministry decisions with reference to church polity or policy?

    1   *2*   *3*   *4*   *5*   *6*   *7*   *8*   *9*   *10*

8. Is it likely that a new member could become chairperson of our official administrative body in less than a year?

    1   *2*   *3*   *4*   *5*   *6*   *7*   *8*   *9*   *10*

9. Do we encourage meetings that last less than an hour?

    1   *2*   *3*   *4*   *5*   *6*   *7*   *8*   *9*   *10*

10. Once we start a new service of worship are we willing to continue it?

    1   *2*   *3*   *4*   *5*   *6*   *7*   *8*   *9*   *10*

11. Are we willing to have a worship service at the same time we have Sunday school?

    1   *2*   *3*   *4*   *5*   *6*   *7*   *8*   *9*   *10*

12. Is the pastor free to preach about or be in involved in moral issues that are also political in nature?

    1   *2*   *3*   *4*   *5*   *6*   *7*   *8*   *9*   *10*

13. Does our church understand that taking strong social stands will not harm the growth of the church?

    1   *2*   *3*   *4*   *5*   *6*   *7*   *8*   *9*   *10*

14. Do we consider worship to be the most important aspect of our ministry?

    1   *2*   *3*   *4*   *5*   *6*   *7*   *8*   *9*   *10*

15. Do we measure the size of our church by the number of people in worship instead of by the actual membership?

    1   *2*   *3*   *4*   *5*   *6*   *7*   *8*   *9*   *10*

16. Do the sermons speak to our personal needs?

    1   *2*   *3*   *4*   *5*   *6*   *7*   *8*   *9*   *10*

17. Does our pastor repeat sermons for no apparent reason?

    1   *2*   *3*   *4*   *5*   *6*   *7*   *8*   *9*   *10*

18. Does Scripture form the basis of the sermons?

    1   *2*   *3*   *4*   *5*   *6*   *7*   *8*   *9*   *10*

19. Do the sermons stimulate thought?

    1   *2*   *3*   *4*   *5*   *6*   *7*   *8*   *9*   *10*

20. Is our worship music pleasing to a majority of the congregation?

    1   *2*   *3*   *4*   *5*   *6*   *7*   *8*   *9*   *10*

21. Is our bulletin the best piece of printed material we produce each week?

    1   *2*   *3*   *4*   *5*   *6*   *7*   *8*   *9*   *10*

22. Do we consider worship to be a form of drama?

    1   *2*   *3*   *4*   *5*   *6*   *7*   *8*   *9*   *10*

23. Do the ushers serve effectively as a team with the pastor or pastors?
   1   2   3   4   5   6   7   8   9   10

24. Are we willing to provide an additional service of worship even though our space may be adequate without it?
   1   2   3   4   5   6   7   8   9   10

25. Do we provide music of high quality at each service?
   1   2   3   4   5   6   7   8   9   10

26. Does our church understand that growth is directly related to the leadership of the pastor?
   1   2   3   4   5   6   7   8   9   10

27. Does our pastor assume leadership for the ministry of our church?
   1   2   3   4   5   6   7   8   9   10

28. Are we willing to provide a pastor with the kind of time away that a long pastorate necessitates?
   1   2   3   4   5   6   7   8   9   10

29. Does our pastor hold up for us a vision large enough to cause us to grow individually?
   1   2   3   4   5   6   7   8   9   10

30. Is our pastor a leader rather than an enabler?
   1   2   3   4   5   6   7   8   9   10

31. Does our pastor cause things to happen in our church that would not happen without his or her instigation?
   1   2   3   4   5   6   7   8   9   10

32. Does our pastor pull us into areas of ministry where we might not go on our own?
   1   2   3   4   5   6   7   8   9   10

33. Does our pastor learn from mistakes?
   1   2   3   4   5   6   7   8   9   10

34. Does our pastor know how to delegate authority, and does he or she do so?
   1   2   3   4   5   6   7   8   9   10

35. Does our pastor consult us regularly about his or her vision for our church?
   1   2   3   4   5   6   7   8   9   10

36. Has our pastor shown the ability to grow and develop new skills as our church grows?
   1   2   3   4   5   6   7   8   9   10

37. Does our pastor possess the skills needed to serve a church our size?
   1   2   3   4   5   6   7   8   9   10

38. Can our pastor respond and relate to a wide variety of religious expressions?
   1   2   3   4   5   6   7   8   9   10

39. Is our pastor able to mediate between the various factions of the church?

      1   *2*   *3*   *4*   *5*   *6*   *7*   *8*   *9*   *10*

40. Does our church have any concrete method of evaluating how long a pastor should stay?

      1   *2*   *3*   *4*   *5*   *6*   *7*   *8*   *9*   *10*

41. Is the main responsibility of our paid staff to identify laity for mission, to recruit, lead, and deploy laity into mission, and to equip laity for mission?

      1   *2*   *3*   *4*   *5*   *6*   *7*   *8*   *9*   *10*

42. Does our pastor make use of the valuable information our paid staff has about the congregation?

      1   *2*   *3*   *4*   *5*   *6*   *7*   *8*   *9*   *10*

43. Do our pastor and paid staff work together as a team?

      1   *2*   *3*   *4*   *5*   *6*   *7*   *8*   *9*   *10*

44. Does our paid staff require minimum supervision?

      1   *2*   *3*   *4*   *5*   *6*   *7*   *8*   *9*   *10*

45. Are we willing to pay higher salaries and be content with fewer paid staff?

      1   *2*   *3*   *4*   *5*   *6*   *7*   *8*   *9*   *10*

46. How would we describe our church in relation to other churches—small, medium, large, or very large? (very large = 1; small = 10)

      1   *2*   *3*   *4*   *5*   *6*   *7*   *8*   *9*   *10*

47. Does our lay leadership communicate to the congregation a realistic perception of our church's size and ability?

      1   *2*   *3*   *4*   *5*   *6*   *7*   *8*   *9*   *10*

48. Does our congregation have a realistic perception of our church's size and ability?

      1   *2*   *3*   *4*   *5*   *6*   *7*   *8*   *9*   *10*

49. Does our lay leadership cause the official vision of the church to materialize in ways that meet the needs of the congregation?

      1   *2*   *3*   *4*   *5*   *6*   *7*   *8*   *9*   *10*

50. Does our lay leadership consider major issues and decisions objectively?

      1   *2*   *3*   *4*   *5*   *6*   *7*   *8*   *9*   *10*

51. Does our lay leadership know the difference between opinion and judgment?

      1   *2*   *3*   *4*   *5*   *6*   *7*   *8*   *9*   *10*

52. Can our lay leadership suspend judgment long enough to make intelligent decisions?

      1   *2*   *3*   *4*   *5*   *6*   *7*   *8*   *9*   *10*

53. Can our lay leadership accept and appreciate people with different viewpoints?

      1   *2*   *3*   *4*   *5*   *6*   *7*   *8*   *9*   *10*

54. Is at least half of our lay leadership new to the institutional church?
    1   2   3   4   5   6   7   8   9   10

55. Is our lay leadership accessible to the rest of the congregation?
    1   2   3   4   5   6   7   8   9   10

56. Does our lay leadership have the necessary time and energy?
    1   2   3   4   5   6   7   8   9   10

57. Does our lay leadership cause things to happen?
    1   2   3   4   5   6   7   8   9   10

58. Does each of our lay leaders have a large following in the congregation?
    1   2   3   4   5   6   7   8   9   10

59. Is the tenure of our lay leadership limited to three years?
    1   2   3   4   5   6   7   8   9   10

60. Does new lay leadership surface on a regular basis?
    1   2   3   4   5   6   7   8   9   10

61. What level of commitment do we expect from our members? High (1)? Medium (5)? Low (10)?
    1   2   3   4   5   6   7   8   9   10

62. Does our church understand that we can use only 80 percent of our space?
    1   2   3   4   5   6   7   8   9   10

63. Do we understand the radical change that has occurred over the past twenty years in the need for parking?
    1   2   3   4   5   6   7   8   9   10

64. Do you have a problem finding a parking space on Sunday morning?
    1   2   3   4   5   6   7   8   9   10

    If so, what hour do you arrive? _____

65. Do we use every event in the life of our church as an entry point for membership?
    1   2   3   4   5   6   7   8   9   10

66. Does our paid and unpaid staff know the importance of Christmas Eve and respond accordingly? (In other words, do we have a service with a choir, ushers, a sermon, and so forth?)
    1   2   3   4   5   6   7   8   9   10

67. Do we have adequate exterior and interior signs posted around the church?
    1   2   3   4   5   6   7   8   9   10

68. Do we have an adequate number of trained hosts and hostesses?
    1   2   3   4   5   6   7   8   9   10

69. When at church, do members go out of their way to meet and welcome people they don't know?

     1   2   3   4   5   6   7   8   9   10

70. Do the members pray regularly that the church will grow spiritually and numerically?

     1   2   3   4   5   6   7   8   9   10

71. Is the appearance of our property pleasing?

     1   2   3   4   5   6   7   8   9   10

72. Does our church talk often about money and financial stewardship?

     1   2   3   4   5   6   7.   8   9   10

73. Do we avoid telling people the church needs their money and instead talk about peoples' need to become stewards?

     1   2   3   4   5   6   7   8   9   10

74. Does our leadership understand the importance of pledge Sunday?

     1   2   3   4   5   6   7   8   9   10

75. What role does the pastor play in the pledge drive?

_____

_____

_____

76. Do we avoid cutting the budget at all costs?

     1   2   3   4   5   6   7   8   9   10

77. Do we look for new ways of raising money each year?

     1   2   3   4   5   6   7   8   9   10

78. Does our church have an overall vision for its ministry and future?

     1   2   3   4   5   6   7   8   9   10

79. What is our church's main strength? (List only one.)

_____

_____

_____

80. What is our church's main weakness? (List only one.)

_____

_____

81. Where is it that our church wants to go?

_____

_____

82. Does our church know what we must do *now* in order to arrive at that destination?

      1   *2*   *3*   *4*   *5*   *6*   *7*   *8*   *9*   *10*

83. What are our short-term objectives?

_____

_____

_____

84. What are our long-term objectives?

_____

_____

_____

85. Do the objectives of our pastor and the church match?

      1   *2*   *3*   *4*   *5*   *6*   *7*   *8*   *9*   *10*

86. Do we hold people accountable?

      1   *2*   *3*   *4*   *5*   *6*   *7*   *8*   *9*   *10*

87. When asking people to do a job, do we let them know that we expect their best?

      1   *2*   *3*   *4*   *5*   *6*   *7*   *8*   *9*   *10*

88. Is our church free from power cliques?

      1   *2*   *3*   *4*   *5*   *6*   *7*   *8*   *9*   *10*

89. Do one or two people derail things that the majority want?

      1   *2*   *3*   *4*   *5*   *6*   *7*   *8*   *9*   *10*

90. What is your age? _____

91. How long have you been a member of this church? _____

OFFICIAL BODY READINESS WORKSHEET

This worksheet is to be completed by *each* member of the church's official body separately. Answers should then be averaged on the total sheet in the Ministry Audit.

CHURCH: _____

DATE: _____

Decide how you *feel* about the following statements, rating your agreement or disagreement with each statement on a scale of one to ten. One means that you totally agree with the statement; ten means that you totally disagree with the statement.

1. The nursery should be extra clean and neat, staffed with paid help, and open every time there is a church function.
   1   2   3   4   5   6   7   8   9   10

2. Turf issues are harmful to the growth of a church.
   1   2   3   4   5   6   7   8   9   10

3. I am willing for the facilities to be used even if they get dirty.
   1   2   3   4   5   6   7   8   9   10

4. Reaching out to new members is just as important as taking care of the present members.
   1   2   3   4   5   6   7   8   9   10

5. I am comfortable with radical change if it will help my church reach more people for Christ.
   1   2   3   4   5   6   7   8   9   10

6. I am seldom concerned about procedure.
   1   2   3   4   5   6   7   8   9   10

7. Paying off the debt is not a major concern to me.

          1   *2*   *3*   *4*   *5*   *6*   *7*   *8*   *9*   *10*

8. I support the idea of spending some of our church's savings in order to hire more staff or start new programs.

          1   *2*   *3*   *4*   *5*   *6*   *7*   *8*   *9*   *10*

9. Several worship services are fine with me because I am more interested in meeting the needs of all the people than I am in knowing everyone at church.

          1   *2*   *3*   *4*   *5*   *6*   *7*   *8*   *9*   *10*

10. I'm not at all offended when my pastor does not give me regular personal attention.

          1   *2*   *3*   *4*   *5*   *6*   *7*   *8*   *9*   *10*

11. I realize that more staff are needed today than in the past.

          1   *2*   *3*   *4*   *5*   *6*   *7*   *8*   *9*   *10*

12. I always trust and affirm my pastor's efforts to reach more people for Christ.

          1   *2*   *3*   *4*   *5*   *6*   *7*   *8*   *9*   *10*

OFFICIAL
BODY PERMISSION GIVING
WORKSHEET

This worksheet is to be completed by *each* member of the church's official body separately. Answers should then be averaged on the total sheet in the Ministry Audit.

CHURCH: _____

DATE: _____

Decide how you *feel* about the following statements, rating your agreement or disagreement with each statement on a scale of one to ten. One means that you totally agree with the statement; ten means that you totally disagree with the statement.

1. Our church leaders believe that people doing the actual ministry should make the majority of the decisions that affect how they do their ministry.

    1   2   3   4   5   6   7   8   9   10

2. People at the lowest level of organization in our church should be able to suggest and implement improvements to their own ministry without going through several committees and levels of approval.

    1   2   3   4   5   6   7   8   9   10

3. Each person in the congregation should be free to live out his or her spiritual gifts in the congregation without getting approval, even if it means starting a new ministry.

    1   2   3   4   5   6   7   8   9   10

4. The nature of ministry lends itself to a team-based approach rather than to individual effort.

    1   2   3   4   5   6   7   8   9   10

5. Our leadership is flexible enough to permit restructuring or reorganization in order to facilitate the new mission of the church.

    1   2   3   4   5   6   7   8   9   10

6. It is possible to organize ministry so that teams can take responsibility for entire ministries.

   1   2   3   4   5   6   7   8   9   10

7. There is enough complexity in our ministry to allow for initiative and decision making.

   1   2   3   4   5   6   7   8   9   10

8. Our leadership is comfortable with individuals or teams making autonomous, on-the-spot decisions.

   1   2   3   4   5   6   7   8   9   10

9. The laity are interested in organizing into teams or small groups or willing to organize into teams or small groups.

   1   2   3   4   5   6   7   8   9   10

10. Our key leadership is willing to share its power with those who are not in leadership.

    1   2   3   4   5   6   7   8   9   10

11. Our church has a history of following through on new ideas.

    1   2   3   4   5   6   7   8   9   10

12. Our key lay leadership is willing to radically change its own roles and behavior.

    1   2   3   4   5   6   7   8   9   10

13. Our church is secure enough to guarantee a period of relative stability during which permission giving can develop.

    1   2   3   4   5   6   7   8   9   10

14. We have adequate resources to support and train our people.

    1   2   3   4   5   6   7   8   9   10

15. Our staff and key lay leadership understand that becoming a permission-giving church is a lengthy, time-consuming, and labor-intensive process that may take five years and is willing to make the investment in time.

    1   2   3   4   5   6   7   8   9   10

16. Our church has a network that could provide information to any layperson anytime.

    1   2   3   4   5   6   7   8   9   10

17. Our laypeople have the skills needed to take greater responsibility for the ministries of the church.

    1   2   3   4   5   6   7   8   9   10

18. Our senior pastor is willing to invest in training the team leaders.

    1   2   3   4   5   6   7   8   9   10

19. Our finance and trustee committees should exist to serve the needs of those trying to implement ministry.

    1   2   3   4   5   6   7   8   9   10

20. Our leaders are more concerned with discovering ways to reach the unchurched than with how those ministries are discovered or implemented.

    1   2   3   4   5   6   7   8   9   10

THE COMPLETE
MINISTRY AUDIT

This is a copy of the blank Ministry Audit that the steering team will fill out and distribute with their report. Make a photocopy of it now so that you can use the blank audit again at another time. Alternately, you can find this document on the bonus software disk under the filename "AUDIT.TXT." After loading the text file as an ASCII document into your word processor, you can edit the questions and develop your answers for easier duplication.

When this document is completed by the team that conducts the audit, it will be distributed to each person who is using the study guide. It will also be distributed with the report when the group is ready to present action possibilities to the congregation.

Two kinds of questions comprise the Ministry Audit: (1) The numbered questions marked by asterisks are to be answered on a scale of 1 to 10, with 1 indicating total agreement or an absolute yes, 10 indicating total disagreement or an absolute no, and the numbers in between indicating degrees of agreement or disagreement. These questions were answered by the official administrative body of the church. They are subjective questions that deal with perception and therefore have no right or wrong answers. I have supplied the average scores for all the questions marked by asterisks. These averages come from the scores of more than two hundred churches throughout the United States. For approximate averages for Canadian churches, add .30 to all of the answers. Any score that is more than .50 above or below the average is outside of the norm for that answer either positively or negatively. (2) The questions that are not marked by asterisks deal with facts more than with perception and are compiled from the various records in the church or from the Worship Survey.

Growth Principle One:
Growth Is Not Concerned with Numbers
but with Meeting the Needs of the People

1. What is the age, gender, and marital status of adult worshipers?
   (Gather this information from the Worship Survey, question 1.)

   M/M = Male/Married, M/S = Male/Single, F/M = Female/Married, F/S = Female/Single

---

BIRTH YEARS

1965–1982	1946–1964	1925–1945	1900–1924
no.: _____	no.: _____	no.: _____	no.: _____
%: _____	%: _____	%: _____	%: _____
M/M_____	M/M_____	M/M_____	M/M_____
M/S _____	M/S _____	M/S _____	M/S _____
F/M _____	F/M _____	F/M _____	F/M _____
F/S _____	F/S _____	F/S _____	F/S _____

Male _____%   Married _____%

Female _____%   Single _____%

How does this compare to the statistics for our area? (Contact the Chamber of Commerce for this information if a Percept demographics profile was not ordered.)

1965–1982	1946–1964	1925–1945	1900–1924
_____%	_____%	_____%	_____%

Based on this comparison, on what age group do we need to concentrate? _____

*2. Does our pastor understand the everyday world of our members? _____ 2.73

3. What are our people programs, including specialized ministries?

_____

_____

_____

4. Has there been any major controversy or division in the past five years?

_____

_____

*5. Does our church deal openly with controversy? _____ 4.81

6. What is our decision-making process?

_____

_____

*7. Do our official administrative body and committee members understand the difference between a working board and an information board? _____ 4.81

*8. If our official administrative body consists of more than twenty-five people, do we have an official executive committee do the basic work? _____ 5.32

*9. Can ministry decisions be made quickly without a lot of red tape? _____ 3.89

*10. Can new members be added to committees and the official administrative body without major delay? _____ 3.02

*11. Do we make the most of our ministry decisions with reference to church polity or policy? _____ 3.24

*12. Is it likely that a new member could become chairperson of our official administrative body in less than a year? _____ 5.83

13. What percentage of the total budget is devoted to programs? (Do not include salaries as program money.) _____

   Is it 10 percent (excluding salaries)? _____

14. Who gives or withholds permission for new ideas or ministries in our church?

   _____

*15. Do we encourage meetings that last less than an hour? _____ 5.78

16. What is our church known for on the community grapevine?

   _____

   _____

17. Describe our church's organizational structure.

   _____

   _____

Growth Principle Two:
Growth Occurs When People Are Given a Wide Variety of Choices

1. Does our church offer a balanced ministry?

   List the various programs under the following headings:

   Love (Nurture)

   _____

   _____

   Justice (Social Action)

   _____

   _____

Mercy (Evangelism)

_____

_____

2. Does our church offer more than one Sunday morning worship service? _____

   At what times? _____   _____   _____

3. If our church offers more than one worship servive, does the same pastor preach each service, or is there a choice? _____

*4. Once we start a new service of worship, are we willing to continue it? _____ 2.83

*5. Are we willing to have a worship service at the same time we have Sunday school? _____ 5.36

6. Does our church have a preschool? _____

   How many attend? _____

7. Does our church have a grade school? _____

   How many attend? _____

8. Does our church have a parent's day out program? _____

   How many attend? _____

9. Does our church have a day care? _____

   How many attend? _____

10. Do we start a new Sunday school class every three to six months? _____

11. Number of adult Sunday school classes: _____

    How many attend? _____

12. Number of singles' Sunday school classes: _____

    How many attend? _____

13. Number of youth Sunday school classes: _____

    How many attend? _____

14. Number of children's Sunday school classes: _____

    How many attend? _____

15. When was the newest adult Sunday school class started? _____

16. Does our church have Sunday evening programs? _____ If so, please list them.

_____

_____

17. Does our church have midweek programs? _____ If so, please list them.

_____

_____

18. Does our church have Bible studies? _____ If so, please list them.

_____

_____

19. Does our church have athletic programs? _____ If so, please list them.

_____

_____

20. List any other programs.

_____

Growth Principle Three:
Growth Occurs When People Are Matched with Their Skills

1. What is our nominating process?

_____

_____

2. Do we encourage and use spiritual gift inventories? _____

Growth Principle Four:
Growth Does Not Dictate That More People Will Become Inactive

1. List the membership figures for the past ten years, beginning with the most recent year.

Year	Membership

2. List our losses in membership for the past ten years, beginning with the most recent year.

Year	Death	Withdrawal	Transfer (to same denom.)	Transfer (to other denom.)	Total

3. Our dropout rate for the past year was _____. (Divide last year's total number of losses into the total membership at the end of the year.) Ten year average is _____.

4. Do we concentrate on assimilating new members within their first three months? _____

5. Is a staff person or a volunteer responsible for assimilation of new members? _____

6. Does our church have enough small groups? _____
   You need one small group for every ten people in worship.

   a. Divide average worship attendance by 10: _____; this is the ideal number of small groups for our church.

   b. Count the number of small groups with fifteen or less in attendance (include Sunday school classes): _____

   c. Subtract line a from line b to determine the number over or under what is needed: _____

7. List the number of each of the following small groups:
   a. Recovery _____
   b. Support _____
   c. Learning _____
   d. Mission or discipling _____
   e. Institutional (required denominational) _____
   f. Sunday school _____

8. How many inactive families do we have? _____

9. What percent of the congregation is inactive? _____

10. Do we have an active program to reinstate our inactives? _____

11. Have we cleaned our rolls within the past three years? _____

12. Describe our assimilation program. _____

_____

_____

Growth Principle Five:
Growth Provides a Wider Outreach to People in Need

1. List the amount of money given to all causes outside our congregation for the past ten years. Include all denominational requirements. List the most recent year first.

Year	Amount Given

Growth Principle Six:
Growth Need Not Be Hampered by Participation in the Public Arena

1. List our programs that are social or political in nature.

_____

_____

*2. How free is the pastor to preach about or be involved in moral issues that are also political in nature? _____ 2.91

*3. Does our church understand that taking strong social stands will not harm the growth of the church? _____ 4.70

Growth Principle Seven:
Growth Will Occur When Worship Is Intentionally Emphasized

*1. Do we consider worship to be the most important aspect of our ministry? _____ 3.59

*2. Do we measure the size of our church by the number of people in worship instead of by the actual membership? _____ 4.48

3. On how many Sundays during the year is there a sermon from our senior pastor? _____

4. On how many Sundays during the year does the service contain a sermon? _____

5. On how many Sundays during the year is there a sermon from our associate pastor? _____

*6. Do the sermons speak to our personal needs? _____ 2.46

*7. Does our pastor repeat sermons for no apparent reason? _____ 9.32

*8. Do scriptures form the basis of the sermons? _____ 1.76

*9. Do the sermons stimulate thought? _____ 2.07

*10. Is our worship music pleasing to a majority of the congregation? _____ 2.00

11. Size of present adult and youth choirs and services at which they sing:

Choir	Service	Present Size	Ideal Size*

*To determine the ideal size for each choir, divide the attendance at the service at which the choir sings by 10.

*12. Is our bulletin the best piece of printed material we produce each week? _____ 3.84

13. What is the percentage of worship attendance to membership? _____

14. Do we have an attendance tracking system? _____

   Do we use it? _____

15. Analysis of worship growth pattern for the past ten years, beginning with the current year:

Year	Average Attendance	Percent Increase (+) or Decrease (−)

Worship has increased/decreased _____ percent in the past ten years.

To determine the percentage of growth or decline each year, take, for example, the amount of difference between year 1 and year 2 and divide it by year 1.

16. Money budgeted for worship: $_____

    Is this 25 percent of the program budget? _____

*17. Do we consider worship to be a form of drama? _____ 6.93

*18. Do the ushers serve effectively as a team with the pastor or pastors? _____ 3.26

Growth Principle Eight:
Growth Will Occur with the Addition of Each New Morning Service of Worship

1. How many morning services of worship do we offer? _____

    At what times? _____

2. Average attendance at each: _____   _____   _____

3. When was the newest service started? _____

*4. Are we willing to provide an additional service of worship even though our space may be adequate without it? _____ 3.10

5. Does each service have a regular choir? _____

6. Is there a youth choir that sings regularly? _____

*7. Do we provide music of high quality at each service? _____ 2.11

8. On how many Sundays per year does our major adult choir sing? _____

9. How many musicals, cantatas, or dramas does our major choir present each year? _____

10. Does our major adult choir take a vacation from singing in church? _____

11. How many children's choirs does our church have? _____

    How often do they sing? _____

12. How many Christmas Eve services does our church have? _____

    Describe each. _____

    _____

    _____

    _____

13. Do we offer worship on a day other than Sunday? _____

Growth Principle Nine:
Growth Is Directly Related to the Leadership Strength of the Pastor

*1. Does our church understand that growth is directly related to the leadership of the pastor? _____
2.64

*2. Does our pastor assume leadership for the ministry of our church? _____ 1.59

3. Average tenure of all senior pastors the past twenty years: _____

4. Tenure of present pastor (or pastors): _____

*5. Are we willing to provide a pastor with the kind of time away that a long pastorate necessitates?
_____ 2.52

6. How much vacation do our pastors and staff receive?

_____

_____

*7. Does our pastor hold up for us a vision large enough to cause us to grow individually? _____ 2.47

*8. Is our pastor a leader rather than an enabler? _____ 2.55

*9. Does our pastor cause things to happen in our church that would not happen without his or her instigation?
_____ 2.05

*10. Does our pastor pull us into areas of ministry where we might not go on our own? _____ 2.51

*11. Does our pastor learn from mistakes? _____ 2.25

*12. Does our pastor know how to delegate authority, and does he or she do so? _____ 2.46

*13. Does our pastor consult us regularly about his or her vision for our church? _____ 2.45

*14. Has our pastor shown the ability to grow and develop new skills as our church grows? _____
2.30

*15. Does our pastor possess the skills needed to serve a church our size? _____ 1.80

*16. Can our pastor respond and relate to a wide variety of religious expressions? _____ 2.01

*17. Is our pastor able to mediate between the various factions of the church? _____ 2.49

*18. Does our church have any concrete method of evaluating how long a pastor should stay? _____
6.14

Growth Principle Ten:
Growth Is Directly Related to the Attitude of the Paid Staff

*1. Is the main responsibility of our paid staff to recruit, lead, and deploy the laity into mission and to equip the laity for mission? _____ 4.97

2. Number of present staff:

Program staff—full-time: _____

Program staff—part-time: _____

Total full-time program staff (add up the part-time people): _____

Support staff—full-time: _____

Support staff—part-time: _____

Total support staff (add up the part-time people): _____

3. Has staff kept pace with growth? _____

4. Is our church staffed for decline, maintenance, or growth (based on the answer to question 2)? _____

5. What is the role of our associate pastor? (Apprentice? Professional? Retired?) _____

*6. Does our pastor make use of the valuable information our paid staff has about the congregation? _____2.74

*7. Do our pastor and paid staff work together as a team? _____ 2.34

8. Does our paid staff have opportunities to develop both relational and functional skills? _____

9. Does our paid staff hold weekly staff meetings? _____

10. Does each paid staff member have an opportunity to have input into the staff agenda? _____

11. Are new ideas from the paid staff welcome at the staff meetings? _____

12. Does the paid staff have yearly retreats? _____

13. Does the paid staff gather on Sunday mornings to go over the day's events (including worship services)? _____

*14. Does our paid staff require minimum supervision? _____ 2.79

*15. Are we willing to pay higher salaries and be content with fewer paid staff? _____ 5.14

16. What percent of our budget do our salaries represent? _____

For churches with less than two hundred in worship, adequate salaries should equal 60 percent of the total budget.

For churches with two hundred or more in worship, adequate salaries should equal 40 percent of the total budget.

17. Does our pastor set aside a certain time each week when individual paid staff members can make appointments to consult with him or her? _____

18. Does our pastor share his or her vision for the congregation at the staff meetings? _____

19. Has our staff had formal training in time management? _____

20. Describe the teaching ministries of our church and the role our staff plays in these ministries.

_____

_____

_____

_____

_____

_____

Growth Principle Eleven:
Growth Is Directly Related to the Unpaid Staff's *Perception* of the Congregation's Size and Ability Rather Than on the Congregation's *Actual* Size and Ability

1. Use the following chart to determine the actual size of our church in relation to other Protestant churches in the United States. For example, if your average worship attendance is 360, your church is larger than 98.4 percent of Protestant churches in the United States.

Average Worship Attendance	Larger Than _____ Percent of Churches
1-49	40.5
50-74	57.5
75-99	69.1
100-149	81.6
150-199	88.6
200-349	96.3
350-499	98.4
500-749	99.3
750-999	99.6
1000 +	99.7

Based on these figures, our church is larger than _____ percent of all Protestant churches. (These figures may vary a few percentage points from denomination to denomination.)

2. How would we describe our church in relation to other churches—small, medium, large, or very large? _____

3. Is our leadership's perception of our church's size the same as the reality of our church's size? (Compare the answer to question 2 to the answer to question 1.) _____

*4. Does our lay leadership communicate to the congregation a realistic perception of our church's size and ability? _____ 4.21

*5. Does our congregation have a realistic perception of our church's size and ability? _____ 4.69

*6. Does our lay leadership cause the official vision of the church to materialize in ways that meet the needs of the congregation? _____ 4.31

*7. Does our lay leadership consider major issues and decisions objectively? _____ 4.13

*8. Does our lay leadership know the difference between opinion and judgment? _____ 3.89

*9. Can our lay leadership suspend judgment long enough to make intelligent decisions? _____ 3.49

*10. Can our lay leadership accept and appreciate people with differing viewpoints? _____ 3.63

*11. Is at least half of our lay leadership new to the institutional church? _____ 6.34

*12. Is our lay leadership accessible to the rest of the congregation? _____ 2.87

*13. Does our lay leadership have the necessary time and energy to carry out its responsibilities? _____ 3.59

*14. Does our lay leadership cause things to happen? _____ 3.57

*15. Do each of our lay leaders have a large following in the congregation? _____ 4.53

*16. Is the tenure of our lay leadership limited to three years? _____ 5.17

*17. Does new lay leadership surface on a regular basis? _____ 4.45

18. What is our greatest challenge in developing lay leaders? (Recruitment? Equipping? Identifying? Deployment?) _____

Growth Principle Twelve:
When 80 Percent of Any Space Is in Use, It Is Time to Start Making Plans for More Space

*1. What level of commitment do we expect from our members? (High? Medium? Low?) _____

2. In the past has our church missed any "windows of opportunity?" _____

*3. Does our church understand that we can use only 80 percent of our space? _____ 6.84

4. Do we need more worship space? _____

(Do not estimate or rely on an architect's estimate. Measure your sanctuary's capacity by actually counting the number of people that can comfortably fit on a pew and multiplying this number by the number of pews in the sanctuary. Alternately, you can measure the total length of all the pews in the sanctuary and divide by 22 inches.)

   a. Sanctuary capacity: _____

   b. Eighty percent capacity: _____

   c. Average attendance at largest service: _____
   (If line c is larger than line b, your church needs more worship space.)

5. Is our worship capacity more than 50 percent larger than our Sunday school capacity? (Compare line 4a, above, with line 8b, below.) _____

6. Do we need more choir space? _____

   a. Choir space capacity: _____

   b. Eighty percent of capacity: _____

   c. Average attendance in the largest choir: _____
   (If line c is larger than line b, the answer to question 6 is yes.)

7. Do we need more nursery space? _____

   a. Nursery capacity: _____

   b. Eighty percent of capacity: _____

   c. Average attendance during the largest service: _____
   (If line c is larger than line b, the answer to question 7 is yes.)

   Number of nursery personnel during the largest service: _____

   Is the nursery available during all events? _____

   Are infants and toddlers separated? _____

   Are there any written nursery policies that are given to the parents? _____

8. Do we need more education space? _____

Allow thirty square feet per person for kindergarten and under; twenty square feet per person for first grade and up. Draw a floor plan for each level of each building and show the capacity of each room and the average attendance of each class. From this figure, calculate the education capacity.

   a. Education capacity: _____

   b. Eighty percent of capacity: _____

c. Average attendance: _____
(If line c is larger than line b, the answer to question 8 is yes.)

9. Is the attendance at each of our Sunday school classes under 80 percent of the capacity for its space?

_____

10. Which classes are filled to over 80 percent of capacity?

_____

_____

Do we need to rearrange any of these classes? _____

11. Number of classrooms available: _____

Number of classrooms presently used: _____

12. Do we offer satellite ministries off of our property? _____

13. List the total Sunday school average attendance and percent of growth for the past ten years, beginning with the current year.

Year	Average Attendance	Percent Increase (+) or Decrease (−)

Sunday school attendance has increased/decreased _____ percent over the past ten years.

14. Do we have more than one session of Sunday school? _____

15. According to the 80 percent rule, does our church need to add space? _____
If so, where?

_____

_____

_____

Growth Principle Thirteen:
Growth Is Encouraged When Parking Is Adequate

1. Does our church own enough land? _____

   If our church owns less than eight acres, is there adjacent property for sale? _____

   We own: _____

   We need: _____

*2. Do we understand the radical change that has occurred over the past twenty years in the need for parking? _____ 3.13

3. What is the average attendance at our largest worship service? (If Sunday school and worship occur at the same hour, count the attendance at both.) _____

4. Average number of people per car: _____

5. Paved off-street parking spaces available (please count): _____

6. Eighty percent of parking capacity: _____

7. Number of spaces needed to accommodate attendance (divide line 3 by line 4): _____

8. How many spaces do we need to add? _____

   (Subtract line 6 from line 7. If line 6 is larger than line 7, no more spaces are needed. Remember: This is an immediate need and does not consider future growth.)

*9. Do you have a problem finding a parking space Sunday morning? _____ 7.28

   If so, what hour do you arrive? _____

Growth Principle Fourteen:
Growth Can Occur Even If the Church Cannot Afford to Build

1. Approximately what would be the yearly debt service on the new facility we need to build? _____

2. What percent of our budget would this be? _____

3. Our total indebtedness is $_____
   (See growth principle 17, question 29)

4. Currently, what percentage of our total budget is our debt service? _____
   (Figure this amount in growth principle 17, question 29).

5. What percentage of our total budget would our debt service be if we were to add a new facility? (Add line 1 to line 4.) _____

6. When was our last building program? _____

7. What did we build? _____

Growth Principle Fifteen:
Growth Can Occur Without Merely Transferring Members from One Church to Another

1. Use the table below to analyze the new membership over the past ten years. How many new members joined by profession of faith? How many transferred from a church of another denomination? How many transferred from a church of the same denomination? (List the current year first.)

Year	Prof. of Faith	Other Denom.	Same Denom.	Total
TOTALS:				

2. Does column 1 outnumber columns 2 and 3? _____

3. Do we intentionally reach out to the unchurched? _____

Answers to questions 4-6 are taken from the Worship Survey.

4. What is the average number of miles our members drive to work? _____

5. What is the average number of minutes our members drive to work? _____

6. What is the average number of miles our members drive to church? _____

If the answer to question 4 is larger than the answer to question 6, concentrate on meeting the needs of the people who drive longer distances to work.

Answers to questions 7, 8, 10, and 12 can be obtained through the Chamber of Commerce or through Percept.

7. How many people live within a ten-mile radius of the church? _____
   Sixty percent of these are unchurched prospects.

8. Who are these unchurched people?
   Singles, never married _____
   Single-parent families _____
   Singles, divorced _____
   Young families _____
   Older families _____
   Middle-aged families _____
   Senior citizens _____
   Black _____
   Brown _____
   White _____
   Yellow _____
   Other _____

9. Which group is not being adequately ministered to in our area? (Call the churches in your area and inquire what programs they offer.)

   _____

   _____

   _____

10. Has the population of our county increased or decreased over the past ten years? _____
    By how much? _____

11. Has our church kept pace with the population increase/decrease of our county? _____

12. Are the schools full in our area? _____

Growth Principle Sixteen:
Growth Almost Always Occurs If the Congregation Is Friendly Toward Visitors

1. How many dollars and what percent of our budget do we devote to the following forms of advertising?

Yellow Pages	$_____
Newspaper	$_____
Flyers	$_____
Radio	$_____
Television	$_____

Direct Mail $_____

Other $_____

TOTAL $_____

PERCENT OF BUDGET _____%

Does the total amount represent 5 percent of our budget? _____

2. a. How many new families visit each week? _____

   b. Do we contact them within forty-eight hours? _____

3. What percent of these families join our church? _____

(Multiply line 2a by 52 and divide that number into the number of new families that join in a year.)

4. What brought these families to our church?

Friends and relatives ____
Driving by ____
Newspaper ____
Yellow pages ____
Preschool ____
Singles' groups ____
Television ____
Banner ____
Direct mail ____
Other ____

5. How many contacts with unchurched people are made each week? _____

6. Does someone on our staff work on behalf of the unchurched twenty hours each week? _____

7. Do we make it clear in worship that we expect visitors each Sunday? _____
   Does our bulletin reflect this? _____

*8. Do we use every event in the life of our church as an entry point for membership? _____ 4.80

9. How many visitors are added to our mailing list each week? _____

10. Do we put visitors on the mailing list the first time they visit? _____

11. Do we promote Christmas Eve services by having adequate space and advertising? _____

*12. Does our paid and unpaid staff know the importance of Christmas Eve and respond accordingly? (In other words, do we have a service with a choir, ushers, a sermon, and so forth?) _____ 1.95

*13. Do we have adequate exterior and interior signs posted around the church? _____ 3.84

*14. Do we have an adequate number of trained hosts and hostesses? _____ 4.95

15. Do we provide colored registration cards for visitors? _____

16. Do we have an evangelism team? _____

17. What group of people or segment of the population can we reach that no one else is ministering to?

_____

18. Do we designate 10 percent of our parking spaces for visitors? _____

19. Do our members wear name tags? _____

20. Does our church have a new members class? _____

21. Do we provide tours of the facilities? _____

*22. When they are at church, do members go out of their way to meet and welcome people they don't know?
_____ 3.99

*23. Do the members pray regularly that the church will grow spiritually and numerically? _____ 4.26

24. Do we provide information packets for visitors? _____

*25. Is the appearance of our property pleasing? _____ 2.03

26. Do we have a booth or a designated area for information? _____
If so, is it well marked? _____

Growth Principle Seventeen:
Asking for Money Encourages Growth

1. List budget totals for the past ten years, including operational and debt service, beginning with the most recent year.

Year	Budget Total

*2. Does our church talk often about money and financial stewardship? _____ 3.94

*3. Do we avoid telling people the church needs their money and instead talk about peoples' need to become stewards? _____ 4.50

4. Is at least one-fourth of our worshiping congregation involved in the preparation for our pledge drives? _____

*5. Does our leadership understand the importance of pledge Sunday? _____ 2.81

6. Do we have a pledge drive every year for the budget? _____

7. At what time of the year is the pledge drive? _____

8. Do we have at least three weeks of education prior to taking pledges? _____

9. Does our pledge card ask only for money? _____

*10. What role does the pastor play in the pledge drive?

_____

_____

11. List the number and average of pledges for the past five years, beginning with the most recent year.

Year	# Pledges	Avg. Amount	Total Pledges	Budget	% of Budget
TOTALS:					

12. Do our pledges underwrite no more than 70 to 90 percent of our budget? _____

13. Has the amount and the number of pledges increased or decreased each year? _____

14. Based on our record, what kind of income can we expect next year if we change nothing?

Pledges from current members $_____

Pledges from new members* $_____

Loose plate offerings $_____

Regular nonpledgers $_____

Building usage fees $_____

Foundation $_____

Special offerings	$_____
Sunday school offerings	$_____
Interest	$_____
Memorials	$_____
Other	$_____
TOTAL	$_____

*If you discount your total pledges from current members to reflect your historical pledge loss, then count your anticipated pledges from new members after you have divided them by 2. If you do not discount the total pledges from current members, then do not count anticipated pledges from new members.

15. Do we select our stewardship leaders on the basis of their giving patterns and willingness to give of themselves? _____

16. Do we contact new members for pledges? _____

17. Do we keep detailed records of giving and pledge patterns and analyze them regularly? _____

18. Is our pledge program centered around tithing? _____

19. How are our stewardship campaigns conducted?

    _____

    _____

20. Describe our past three stewardship programs.

    _____

    _____

    _____

21. Do we encourage designated giving and discourage a unified budget? _____

22. Does our pledge card offer us choices? _____

23. Does our Christmas offering equal at least one-half of one month's income? _____

24. Do we personalize our pledge program? _____

25. Do we have regular special offerings for items within the budget? _____

26. Complete the first chart on page 123 for the past ten years, beginning with the most recent year.

27. Does our total budget income (operating and building) equal or exceed $1,000 for every person in worship on an average Sunday? (See chart.) _____

28. Does one-third of our church's income come from no more than one-fourth of our pledges? _____

29. Complete the second chart on page 123 (on indebtedness) for the past ten years, beginning with the most recent year.

Year	Average Worship Attendance	Percent of Budget to Average Worship Attendance*	Percent of Budgeted Income to Average Worship Attendance**

*Divide worship total into budget total for each year.
**Divide worship total into budgeted income total for each year. Budgeted income is the actual amount the church received—not what it budgeted.

Year	Total Indebtedness	Indebtedness: Percent of Budget*	Budgeted Debt Service (mortgage)	Debt Service: Percent of Budget**
TOTALS:				

*Divide budget total into indebtedness total for each year.
**Divide budget total into budgeted debt service total for each year.

30. Is our debt service under 25 percent of our total operating budget? (See chart.) _____

31. List of financial resources:

Endowments	$_____
Wills	$_____
Capital fund pledges	$_____
Cash reserves	$_____
Foundation	$_____
Stocks and bonds	$_____
Other	$_____
TOTAL	$_____

32. Is there a plan to use this money? _____

33. Before we retire a mortgage do we designate a new ministry to use the same amount of money we have been using to pay the mortgage? _____

34. Do we allow the use of plaques that recognize those who have given generously? _____

*35. Do we avoid cutting the budget at all costs? _____ 5.22

*36. Do we look for new ways of raising money each year? _____ 4.83

37. When was our last capital funds drive? _____

38. Does our pastor know what each member gives? _____

Growth Principle Eighteen: Growth Can Be Long-Term If a Solid Foundation Has Been Laid

*1. Does our church have an overall vision for its ministry and its future? _____ 3.54

2. Does our church have a mission statement that is clear, concise, and open-ended? _____

3. Does our church have a logo other than our denominational logo? _____

4. Does our church have an anthem? _____

5. If we do have a logo and an anthem, are they used consistently? _____

6. Do we have a regularly updated five- or ten-year plan? _____

7. Do we have a master plan for the use of land and facilities? _____

8. When was the last time we did strategic planning? _____

*9. What is our church's main strength? (List only one.)

_____

_____

*10. What is our church's main weakness? (List only one.)

_____

_____

Growth Principle Nineteen:
Regular Strategic Planning Is Necessary for Growth to Be Healthy

*1. Where is it that our church wants to go?

_____

_____

*2. Does our church know what we must do *now* in order to arrive at that destination? _____ 5.23

3. List present officially adopted objectives or goals of the church.

_____

_____

_____

*4. What are our short-term objectives?

_____

_____

_____

*5. What are our long-term objectives?

_____

_____

*6. Do the objectives of our pastor and those of the church match? _____ 2.65

*7. Do we hold people accountable? _____ 5.23

*8. When asking people to do a job, do we let them know that we expect their best? _____ 4.36

9. Do we evaluate each program or strategy? _____

Growth Principle Twenty:
It Takes More Effort to Implement Change Than to Maintain the Status Quo or to Exercise Veto Power

*1. Is our church free from power cliques? _____ 6.20

*2. Do one or two people derail things that the majority want? _____ 6.38

*3. What is the average age of the person filling out this report? _____ (average among two hundred churches surveyed: 52)

*4. What is the average length of time the person filling out the Official Body Worksheet has been a member? _____ (average among two hundred churches surveyed: 18)

5. How many people received the Official Body Worksheet? _____

6. How many people completed the Official Body Worksheet? _____

7. Do we make any changes in our schedule in the summer? _____

If so, what are they?

_____

_____

Section Four

AFTER THE STUDY

THE REPORT

Make a Diagnosis

In making this report, you are functioning more as a physician than as a counselor. Physicians make a diagnosis and then write a prescription. Neither is a value judgment, but is as accurate a reading of the church's condition and recommended course of action as possible.

Decide on the type of report you are going to make—dated recommendations or trigger points. I do not recommend that you do this study and then fail to make some form of definite recommendations.

Measurable, Dated, and Simple Recommendations

Example: By September of 1997, establish a contemporary service during church school that uses very little liturgy, stresses praise choruses, and uses a synthesizer and drums.

Trigger Points Tell Us When to Do What

Example: When our largest worship service reaches 80 percent capacity, it is time to begin planning for a third worship service during the Sunday school hour.

Make the Presentation to the Official Body

Charts are essential. Following are examples of types of charts that would be helpful when making your presentation to the official body.

MEMBERSHIP/ATTENDANCE
X Church, Any City

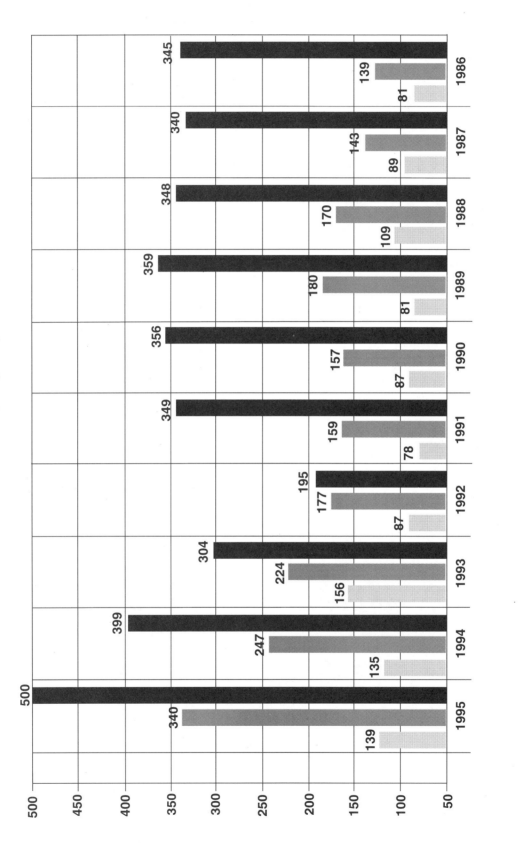

Membership

Worship Attendance

Sunday School Attendance

	1986	1987	1988	1989	1990	1991	1992	1993	1994	1995
Membership	345	340	348	359	356	349	195	304	399	500
Worship Attendance	139	143	170	180	157	159	177	224	247	340
Sunday School Attendance	81	89	109	81	87	78	87	156	135	139

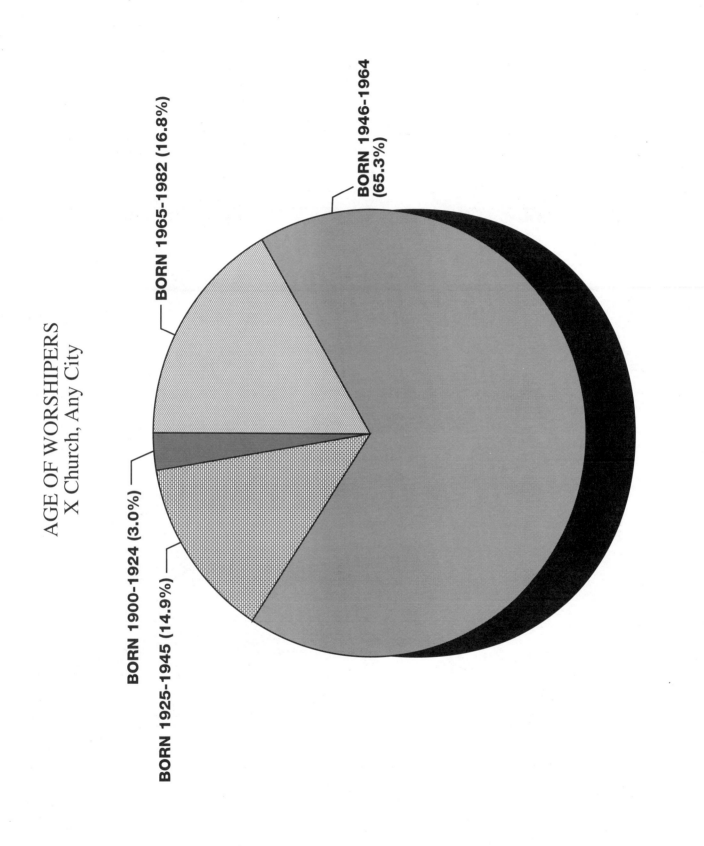

AGE OF WORSHIPERS
X Church, Any City

BORN 1965-1982 (16.8%)

BORN 1946-1964
(65.3%)

BORN 1900-1924 (3.0%)

BORN 1925-1945 (14.9%)

NEW MEMBERS/LOSSES
X Church, Any City

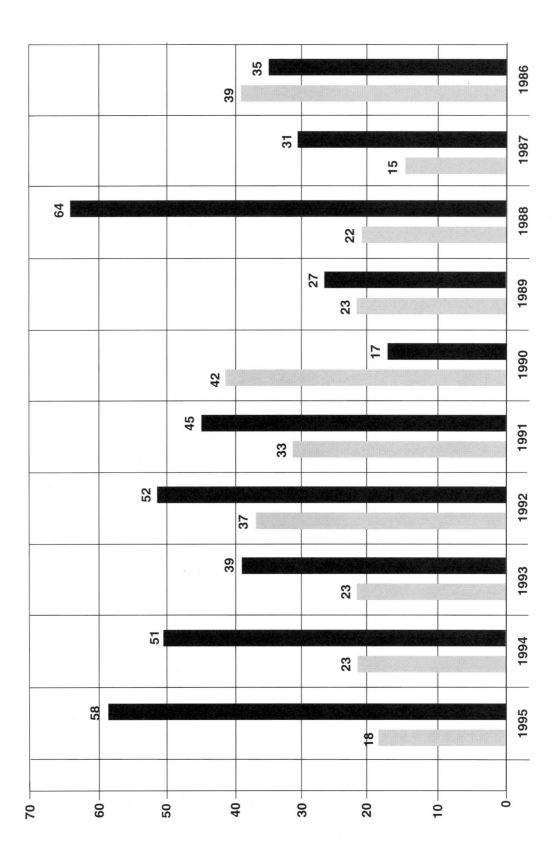

Losses ■

New Members ▨

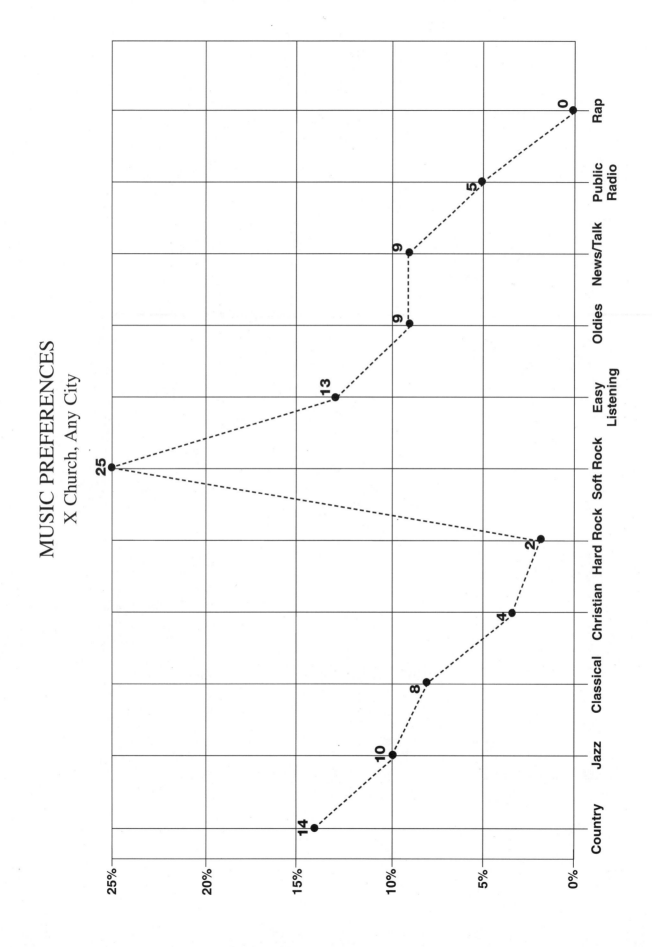

MUSIC PREFERENCES
X Church, Any City

READINESS CHART
X Church, Any City

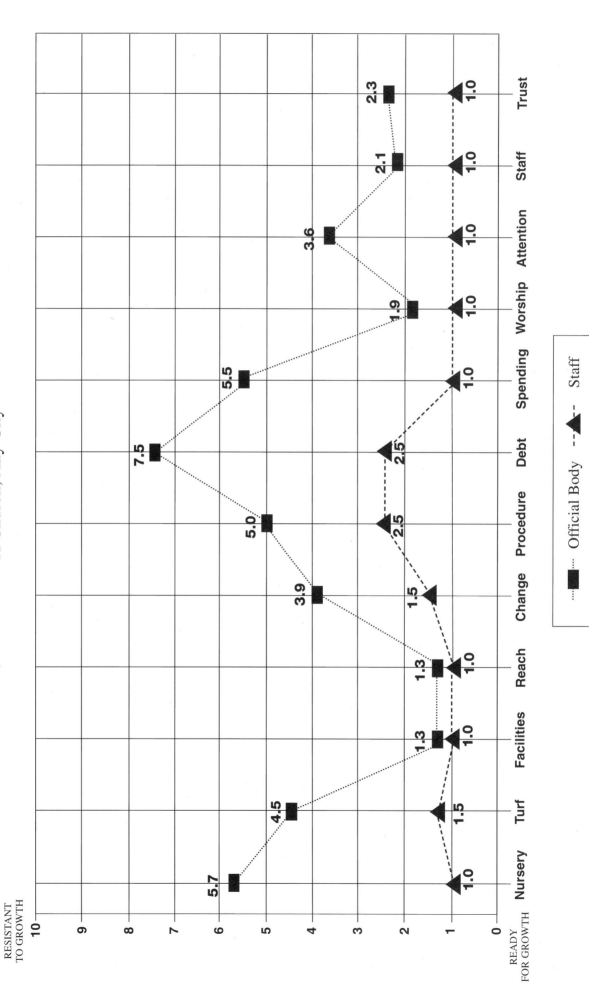

RESISTANT TO GROWTH — 10

READY FOR GROWTH — 0

Legend: Official Body · · · · ■ · · · · Staff - - - ▲ - - -

Nursery 5.7, 1.0
Turf 4.5, 1.5
Facilities 1.3, 1.0
Reach 1.3, 1.0
Change 3.9, 1.5
Procedure 5.0, 2.5
Debt 7.5, 2.5
Spending 5.5, 1.0
Worship 1.9, 1.0
Attention 3.6, 1.0
Staff 2.1, 1.0
Trust 2.3, 1.0

Give a completed copy of the Ministry Audit to all church leaders prior to any meeting regarding the report.

Have several or all of the planning team make portions of the presentation.

Avoid using too many statistics, especially in discussing the demographics.

Never vote on an issue the first time you meet to discuss it.

Meet from 7:00 to 9:00 in the evening with no break. Make sure the nursery is open and staffed so that the younger members can attend.

Always begin with a few very positive statements about the church.

Tell those to whom you are presenting the report that you are going to share with them what they have taught you about their church.

Step One: Introducing the Report

1. Begin by praising the official body for one or two things.
2. Move quickly to a time of spiritual reflection. This is a time of motivation.
3. Push the official body to think outward, rather than inward.
4. Make reference to one or more Bible passages (see section 2: The Basic Law of Congregational Life) and be sure to ground your time in solid theology. This time needs to be as much a revival as a lecture about their church and community.
5. Drop hints about the things that are hindering growth. Use humor when possible.

Step 2: Presenting Your Findings

1. Familiarize the official body with the Ministry Audit but do not go over the audit piece by piece. Use only what is important to your church.
2. Make sure the official body understands how the Ministry Audit was put together.
3. Hit the high points.
4. Use graphs or charts. The more visual aids the better. If you are going to use visual aids, you will need an overhead projector and screen. Make sure the words on the transparencies are large enough to be read from the back of the room. The fewer words the better.
5. Avoid being technical.
6. Explain each of the twenty principles that is relevant to your particular church.

Step 3: Presenting Your Recommendations

1. Hand out your recommendations in written form.
2. Make sure everyone understands that these recommendations are the groundwork for future dialogue and decision.
3. Go over the recommendations and let the people ask questions. Avoid defending or arguing the recommendations.

Step 4: Concluding the Report

1. Close with some inspirational story that brings together all the pieces.
2. Leave time to turn it over to the pastor to close the meeting.
3. Arrange an appropriate closing ahead of time with the pastor.
4. Always make sure that the next step in the process is set in place before the meeting adjourns.

Choose a Process for Moving the Report from Recommendation to Implementation

Your report must be processed through the congregation and revised and refined as you go if it is to reflect the values of the leadership and have a chance of being implemented. Spend all the time necessary to process the material, but remember that there is a limit to the enthusiasm any large group will give to a process before they begin to lose interest. As you go further into the process, more and more of the congregation should have the opportunity to be involved. You will find the process I used through much of my ministry in my book *Sacred Cows Make Gourmet Burgers*, especially in chapter 11 (see Recommended Reading).

It is absolutely essential that the key leaders feel good about the recommendations and are willing to share their enthusiasm with the congregation. They must be willing to interpret the recommendations and stand up for them when opposition arises.

The leadership needs to understand that anytime a church attempts to do anything important or to make the strategic adjustments necessary to meet the demands of a new generation, it always has a few members who strongly oppose such change, if for no other reason than "we have never done it that way before." To give in to these vocal few results in hurting many unseen people by not ministering to their needs. Some people will get upset about your recommendations. That is the case in every situation. Do your best to bring them along in your planning and decision making, but do not allow such opposition to stop the momentum. By the time you finish the process described in *Sacred Cows Make Gourmet Burgers*, the vast majority of the leaders of your church will be ready to move positively on all the amended recommendations. May God bless your efforts as you seek to respond faithfully to the human and spiritual needs around your church and throughout the world.

If you would like William Easum to analyze your Ministry Audit, he will do so (for a fee). Reach him by phone, at (512)749-5364; fax, at (512)749-5364; or e-mail, at easum@aol.com.

RECOMMENDED RESOURCES

The following resources are recommended because of their ability to equip the laity and reach the unchurched.

Administration

1. Schaller, Lyle E. *The Larger Church and the Multiple Staff*. Nashville: Abingdon, 1980.

2. For "Personnel Policies and Procedures" or "Job Descriptions," write Multi-Staff Ministries, 17616 Arvida Drive, Granada Hills, CA 91344. Phone or fax 818-360-8187. This information comes in both print and disk form.

3. *Administration and Restructuring* includes sample job descriptions for Executive Administrator, Minister of Programs, Music Director, and Minister of Youth and samples of record keeping for vital ministries. 21st Century Strategies, Inc., 1126 Whispering Sands, Port Aransas, TX 78373. Phone 512-749-5364; fax 512-749-5800. $7.00.

4. *Leadership Development for the 1990s* is a complete guide to developing leadership with an emphasis on vision casting. 21st Century Strategies, Inc., 1126 Whispering Sands, Port Aransas, TX 78373. Phone 512-749-5364; fax 512-749-5800. $7.00.

5. *Developing a Multiple Staff* includes information on developing a staff as well as helpful hints I have learned from practical experience. 21st Century Strategies, Inc., 1126 Whispering Sands, Port Aransas, TX 78373. Phone 512-749-5364; fax 512-749-5800. $5.00.

Adults

1. "Growth Principles and Methods for Adult Sunday School Classes," available from Net Results Resource Center, 5001 Avenue N, Lubbock, TX 79412-2993. Phone 806-762-8094.

2. "Super eight suppers" are described in the "Additional Resources Packet" available from Net Results Resource Center, 5001 Avenue N, Lubbock, TX 79412-2993. Phone 806-762-8094.

3. Murray, Dick. *Teaching the Bible to Adults and Youth*. Nashville: Abingdon, 1993.

Assimilation

1. For churches that do not become small-group-based, ask Net Results for Reprint Pacs 7015, 7016, 7028, 7021. Net Results Resource Center, 5001 Avenue N, Lubbock, TX 79412-2993. Phone 806-762-8094.
2. Mathison, John Ed. *Every Member in Ministry Involving Laity and Inactives*. Nashville: Discipleship Resources, 1988.

Bible Studies

1. *DISCIPLE*. Contact Wini Grizzle, Room 233, P.O. Box 801, Nashville, TN 37202.
2. Bethel Series. P.O. Box 8395, Madison, WI 53708.
3. Kerygma Program. 300 Mt. Lebanon Blvd., Suite 205, Pittsburgh, PA 15234.
4. Trinity Bible Studies. Box 77, El Paso, AR 72045.
5. Through the Bible in One Year. 6116 East 32nd Street, Tulsa, OK 74135.

Children

1. Logos Program, Inc. 1405 Frey Road, Pittsburgh, PA 15235. This is an excellent program for an after-school or evening ministry for elementary-school-aged children.
2. *Bible Paint & Learn II*, a series of electronic coloring books for children 4 to 8, available from ARK Multimedia Publishing, 323 W. Mercury Blvd., Hampton, VA 23666. Phone 804-838-2807.
3. Pioneer Clubs offers good material for those who want a conservative approach. Write them at Box 788, Wheaton, IL 60189-0788. Phone 708-293-1600.

Church Planting, Building, and Relocating

1. Schaller, Lyle E. *44 Questions for Church Planters*. Nashville: Abingdon, 1991.
2. Malkoff and Associates are project managers. They also help churches deal with the city or state government regarding restrictions, zoning, or anything that stands in the way of building, expanding, or relocating. They are the primary firm that helped Saddleback Church through its fifty-two moves. Write them at 417 Tustin Avenue, Suite 100, Newport Beach, CA 92663. Phone 1-800-MALKOFF; fax 714-574-7453.

Computers

1. *Christian Computing*, a magazine, is a good source for information about electronic resources for churches and Christian educators. To order, write to Christian Computing, Inc., P.O. Box 198, 406 Pine Street Center, Suite L-M, Raymore, MO 64083. Phone 816-331-3881; fax 816-331-5510.
2. Shelby Systems makes software designed to handle churches of all sizes. It has everything you need. It is expensive and requires extensive training, but you will never outgrow it. To order, write to Shelby Systems, 65 Germantown Court, Suite 303, Cordova, TN 38018. Phone 913-877-0222.
3. *Bible Paint & Learn II*, a series of electronic coloring books for children 4 to 8, available from ARK Multimedia Publishing, 323 W. Mercury Blvd., Hampton, VA 23666. Phone 804-838-2807.
4. Future Vision Software produces family-oriented programs that can be used by any or all of the family, with interactive and individual applications. Phone 1-800-359-9169.
5. Desktop Ministry offers a variety of good software products for program use. Their electronic brochure for use in the foyer on Sunday is very good. You can order samples by calling 1-800-964-5250; or write to Desktop Ministry, Emerald Blvd., Southlake, TX 76092.

6. Wisdom Tree, Inc. has software games that help children learn the Bible. Phone 1-800-772-4253.

7. Bridgestone Multimedia group has software games that help children learn the Bible. 979 Palomar Oaks Way, Carlsbad, CA 92009.

8. Computers with 286 or 386 chips can be upgraded by adding a 486 chip from Buffalo Products, Inc. Ask for their 486 Powerkit. The cost is $149 for a 386 and $259 for the 286. You will have to install the chip or get someone to do it for you. 1-800-345-2356.

Conflict Management

1. Leas, Speed B. *How to Deal Constructively with Clergy/Lay Conflict*. Washington, D.C.: Alban Institute, 1987.

2. Haugk, Kenneth. *Antagonists in the Church*. Nashville: Abingdon, 1988.

3. John Savage, L.E.A.D. Consultants, Box 664, Reynoldsburg, OH 43068. Phone 614-864-0156. This group provides some of the best small group and listening skills training anywhere. Their methods for dealing with conflict management are the best I have seen.

Demographics

1. To order an easily understandable demographic report for your area from Percept, write Stanley Menking at Perkins School of Theology, Southern Methodist University, Box 133, Dallas, TX 75275. Phone 214-768-2251.

2. *American Demographics* is a monthly magazine that describes trends in the United States as they are developing. Phone 1-800-828-1133.

3. Menking, Stanley J. *Demographics Workshop Handbook*. Dallas: Perkins School of Theology at SMU, Continuing Education Department, 1991. To order, write to Perkins School of Theology at SMU, Box 133, Dallas, TX 75275-0133; or call 214-768-2251. $10.00.

4. Templeton, Jane. *Focus Groups: A Guide for Marketing and Advertising Professionals*. Ithaca, N.Y.: American Demographic, DATE. To order, write to American Demographics, P.O. Box 68, Ithaca, NY 14851, or call 1-800-828-1133.

5. Barna, George. *Church Marketing*. Ventura, Calif.: Regal Books, 1992. Provides more information about focus groups.

Direct Mail

1. Mueller, Walter. *Direct Mail Ministry*. Nashville: Abingdon, 1989.

2. For technical advice on mass mailings, contact the Rev. Deral Schrom, South Suburban Christian Church, 7175 South Broadway, Littleton, CO 80122.

3. Petrogram provides graphics for direct mail. The Petrogram Group, 1318 Jamestown Rd., Suite 202, Williamsburg, VA 23185. Phone 804-220-1877.

Evangelism

1. There are several good inexpensive sources for finding new residents: Research Data, Inc., 16950 Dallas Parkway, Dallas, TX 75248. Dataman Information Services, Inc., 1100 Johnson Ferry Rd., Suite 450, Atlanta, GA 30342. New Resident Data Marketing, Inc., phone 201-666-2212. When requesting information about your area, do not forget to include the county or counties served by your church.

2. The popular program "Bring a Friend" can be ordered from Net Results in Reprint Pac "Finding Prospective New Members." Net Results Resource Center, 5001 Avenue N, Lubbock, TX 79412-2993. Phone 806-762-8094.

3. Brueggemann, Walter. *Biblical Perspectives on Evangelism: Living in a Three-Storied Universe*. Nashville: Abingdon, 1993. The best book in print at the moment on the relationship of evangelism to the Judeo-Christian biblical traditions. It also offers a very good word on the relationship between evangelism and social justice.

4. Miller, Herb. *How to Build a Magnetic Church*. Nashville: Abingdon, 1987.

5. "The Phone Is for You," can be ordered from Church Growth Development International, 420 W. Lambert Rd., Suite E, Brea, CA 92621. Phone 717-990-9551. For help designing the mail-outs, see Petrogram (item 3 under Direct Mail).

6. *Evangelism and Assimilation* includes sample letters and programs used at Colonial Hills United Methodist Church as well as an outline for responding to first-time visitors, information on banners, direct mail, and personal networks. 26 pages. 21st Century Strategies, Inc., 1126 Whispering Sands, Port Aransas, TX 78373. Phone 512-749-5364; fax 512-749-5800. $5.00.

7. Easum, William M. *The Church Growth Handbook*. Nashville: Abingdon, 1990.

8. Easum, William M. *How to Reach Baby Boomers*. Nashville: Abingdon, 1991.

Family Ministries

1. The Stepfamily Association of America, phone 402-477-7837.
2. National Center for Fathering, 217 Southwind Place, Manhattan, KS 66502. Phone 913-776-4114.
3. Friedman, Edwin. *Generation to Generation*. New York: Guilford Press, 1985.

Futuring

1. Mead, Loren. *The Once and Future Church*. Washington, D.C.: Alban Institute, 1991. The Alban Institute, 4125 Nebraska Avenue NW, Washington, D.C., 20016. This is required reading for churches wishing to establish new ministries for the twenty-first century.

2. Toffler, Alvin. *Power Shift*. New York: Bantam Books, 1990.

3. Naisbitt, John and Patricia Aburdene. *Megatrends 2000*. New York: Morrow, 1990.

4. Barker, Joel. *Future Edge*. New York: Morrow, 1992.

5. Easum, William M. *Dancing with Dinosaurs*. Nashville: Abingdon, 1993.

6. *Ministry in a Changing World* is a twelve-hour audio cassette seminar with a workbook in one carrying case. 141 pages. 21st Century Strategies, Inc., 1126 Whispering Sands, Port Aransas, TX 78373. Phone 512-749-5364; fax 512-749-5800. $69.95.

7. *Transforming Congregations* is a three-hour video with an accompanying workbook. 30 pages. 21st Century Strategies, Inc., 1126 Whispering Sands, Port Aransas, TX 78373. Phone 512-749-5364; fax 512-749-5800. $69.95.

General

1. *Net Results*, a magazine covering issues of church leadership, vitality, ideas, and methods, is available from Net Results Resource Center, 5001 Avenue N, Lubbock, TX 79412-2993. Phone 806-762-8094.

Inactives

1. John Savage, L.E.A.D. Consultants, Box 664, Reynoldsburg, OH 43068. Phone 614-864-0156. Savage is the leading authority on regaining inactives.

2. "Coming Home for Christmas," a pamphlet by Herb Miller, is part of the Reprint Pac "Reactivating Inactive Members," available through Net Results Resources, 5001 Avenue N, Lubbock, TX 79412-2993. Phone 806-762-8094.

Lay Ministries—Small Group Ministries (The Meta Model)

1. Arnold, Jeffery. *Starting Small Groups* (Nashville: Abingdon, 1997).
2. "How to Identify Your Spiritual Giftabilities," in Reprint Pac "Creating a Positive Congregational Climate." Net Results Resources, 5001 Avenue N, Lubbock, TX 79412-2993. Phone 806-762-8094.
3. "Networking" is a comprehensive spiritual gift study program developed by the Fuller Institute, Box 919901, Pasadena, CA 91109. Phone 1-800-999-9578. Developed around the Willow Creek model. $67.95.
4. Program-based churches wishing to become small-group-based churches may contact North Star Strategies, 1500 N. Lincoln, Urbana, IL 61801, in care of Jim Egli. Phone 217-384-3070.
5. Galloway, Dale. *20/20 Vision*. Portland: Scott Publishing, 1986.
6. George, Carl. *Prepare Your Church for the Future*. New York: Fleming H. Revell, 1991.
7. *Small Group Church* is a monthly magazine produced by Touch Ministries, 14925 Memorial Drive, Suite 101, Houston, Texas 77079.
8. "First Love," a video from Ginghamsburg United Methodist Church detailing its small group ministry based on the Meta model. Media Resources for Ministry, United Theological Seminary, 1810 Harvard Blvd., Dayton, OH 45406. Phone 1-800-322-5817; inside Ohio, phone 1-800-686-HOPE.
9. Stephen Ministry has developed a new ministry for small groups that can be used in program-based churches that do not wish to become cell-based churches. Stephen Ministry, 8016 Dale, St. Louis, MO 63117. Phone 314-645-5511.
10. Birkman & Associates, Inc. can help you in the selection of staff and key laity to lead in important positions. They are a worldwide management consulting firm that is now interested in helping churches select and train leadership. 3040 Post Oak Blvd., Suite 1425, Houston, Texas 77056. Phone 713-623-2760.
11. Mathison, John Ed. *Every Member in Ministry Involving Laity and Inactives*. Nashville: Discipleship Resources, 1988.
12. "Pastor's Update and Shared Ministry," an audio cassette that comes monthly, with up-to-date lessons learned about the Meta model. Fuller Institute, Box 919901, Pasadena, CA 91109. Phone 1-800-999-9578. This may or may not be available in the future, but the back copies are great.
13. *Walking with God*, an excellent print series for small group ministries, from Willow Creek Community Church in South Barrington, Illinois. Grand Rapids, Mich.: Zondervan.
14. "Small Group Leaders Training Manual" is an excellent booklet that gives examples of all of the major small group ministry models. To order write to Serendipity, Box 1012, Littleton, CO 80160; or call 1-800-525-9563.
15. The 2:7 Series from Navigators, P.O. Box 6000, Colorado Springs, CO 80934.
16. Wilson, Marlene. *How to Mobilize Church Volunteers*. Minneapolis: Augsburg, 1983.
17. John Savage, L.E.A.D. Consultants, Inc., Box 664, Reynoldsburg, OH 43068. Phone 614-864-0156. Savage is an excellent trainer for lay ministries.
18. Hestenes, Roberta. *Using the Bible in Groups*. Minneapolis: Westminster, 1985.
19. Hamline, Judith. *Curriculum and Resources for Small Groups* and *The Small Group Leaders Training Course*. Colorado Springs: NavPress, 1992. Phone 1-800-366-7788.
20. Paul Galloway, Telecare Ministries, Fuller Institute, Box 919901, Pasadena, CA 91109. Phone 1-800-999-9578. $22.95.
21. Becker, Palmer. *Called to Equip*. Scottdale, Pa.: Herald Press, 1993.
22. Equipping Ministries, International, has a good catalogue of materials. 4015 Executive Park Drive, Suite 309, Cinncinnati, OH 45241. Phone 513-769-5353.
23. "Nine Facets of Effective Small Group Leaders" (video), with Carl George. Center for Development of

Leadership for Ministry, 231 Indian Creek Road, P.O. Box 5407, Diamond Bar, CA 91765; phone 909-396-6843.

24. *52 Ministry Skills for Small Group Leaders* describes the training of laity by the four district pastors of New Hope Community Church in Portland, Oregon (The latest small group ministry in North America). It includes fifty-two practical lessons accompanied by a one-hour tape of an actual training session. Foundation of Hope, 11731 S.E. Stevens Road, Portland, OR 79266. Phone 1-800-935-4673. $69.95.

25. *Cell Church* is a monthly magazine. To order a copy or to subscribe, write to Cell Church, 14925 Memorial Drive, Suite 101, Houston, TX 77079.

26. *Discovering Our Place in God's World* is a workbook on spiritual gifts. It contains a spiritual gift inventory for mainline churches, an outline of a retreat using the inventory, definitions of spiritual gifts, and more. 52 pages. 21st Century Strategies, Inc., 1126 Whispering Sands, Port Aransas, TX 78373. Phone 512-749-5364, fax 512-749-5800. $15.00.

27. *L.I.F.E. Groups* is a handbook for a small group ministry based on the meta model and designed to work in churches at any place on the theological spectrum. 104 pages. 21st Century Strategies, Inc., 1126 Whispering Sands, Port Aransas, TX 78373. Phone 512-749-5364; fax 512-749-5800. $20.00.

28. *UMCR-Cell Ministry* is a handbook for a small group ministry currently being used at United Methodist Church of the Resurrection in Lionville, Pennsylvania. It is a good example of how small group ministries can be adapted to fit any organizational structure. 51 pages. 21st Century Strategies, Inc., 1126 Whispering Sands, Port Aransas, TX 78373. Phone 512-749-5364; fax 512-749-5800. $10.00.

Marketing

1. Barna, George. *Church Marketing*. Ventura, Calif.: Regal Books, 1992.
2. Shawchuck, Norman, et al. *Marketing for Congregations*. Nashville: Abingdon, 1992.

Music—Contemporary

1. Hosanna Integrity Music, P.O. Box 16813, Mobile, AL 36616. Phone 1-800-877-4443.
2. Maranatha! Music. Phone 1-800-444-4012 or 1-800-245-7664.
3. Saddleback Praises. Phone 1-800-458-2772
4. Brentwood Music (slides; see item 10). Phone 1-800-333-9000.
5. Bethel Chapel, Box 51, Brentwood, TN 37024.
6. Christian Copyright Licensing, Inc., 6130 N.E. 78th, Suite C-11, Portland, OR 97218. The charge is based on the size of the church.
7. Word Music offers an excellent book on planning worship called *Songs for Praise and Worship: Worship Planner Edition*. This material is a must for those planning contemporary worship designed around a theme. Phone 1-800-933-9673, ext. 2389, 2784, 2374.
8. J & J Graphics and Designs (slides; see item 10), 39888 John Drive, Canton, MI 48187. Phone 313-453-0697; fax 313-453-0698.
9. WellSprings Unlimited, Inc., 204 Stevens Court, Burnsville, MN 55306. Phone 612-890-6123. This is a new music ministry for mainline Protestants, and much of it includes inclusive language. The music is good but low-key and is designed by two United Methodist leaders.
10. I do not know of a publisher other than WellSprings Unlimited that offers slides that use inclusive language. One option is to purchase the music and the copyright and then make your own slides or overhead transparencies using inclusive language. If you use slides, make the background black and the words white (reverse the negative) so that it will be legible in the daytime. Overheads show up better during the day, but they are generally more distracting during worship.

New Residents

1. GGC Associates, Inc., 2900 Bristol, Bldg. H, Suites 202-203, Costa Mesa, CA 92626. Phone 1-800-444-9521. They can provide both names and sample letters to mail to the various kinds of new residents.

2. Weeks, Andrew. *Welcome*. Washington D.C.: Alban Institute, 1992. Alban Institute, 4125 Nebraska Avenue, N.W., Washington, DC 20016. Phone 1-800-457-2674. $15.95

Newsletter

1. De Vries, Charles. *Religious Public Relations Handbook*. Religious Public Relations Council, Inc., P.O. Box 315, Gladwyne, PA 19035.

Nursery

1. *Crib, Crawl, Walk: A Nursery for Our Time* has excellent suggestions for making a quality nursery. 20 pages. 21st Century Strategies, Inc., 1126 Whispering Sands, Port Aransas, TX 78373. Phone 512-749-5364; fax 512-749-5800. $5.00.

Pastoral Care

1. *Care Notes*, pamphlets aimed at helping those who hurt in mind, in body, or in spirit, offer a blend of information and inspiration, modern psychology and religion. *Care Notes* cover the gamut of pastoral counseling needs. Abbey Press, One Caring Place, St. Meinrad, IN 47577

Prayer

1. *Prayer Tract News*, Global Harvest Ministries, 215 N. Marengo Avenue, Suite 151, Pasadena, CA 91101. Phone 818-577-7122.

Singles

1. Britton Wood. *How to Start a Singles Ministry*. Nashville: Broadman, 1986.

2. Murren, Doug. *The Baby Boomerang*. Ventura, Calif.: Regal Books, 1990.

3. Dodd, J. Kenneth. *Beyond the Storm of Separation and Divorce*. A set of six audio tapes with workbooks and a leader's guide. Bracken Life Resources, 2320 East Matthews, Suite 226, Jonesboro, AK 72401.

4. National Single Adult Ministries Resource Directory, 1991/92, NavPress, P.O. Box 35001, Colorado Springs, CO 80934.

Small Churches

1. *The Small Church* is a booklet designed for churches with less than one hundred in worship. 44 pages. 21st Century Strategies, Inc., 1126 Whispering Sands, Port Aransas, TX 78373. Phone 512-749-5364; fax 512-749-5800. $10.00.

Social Justice

1. Industrial Areas Foundation. Call 512-222-8562 (San Antonio office) for information.

2. Several good software programs designed to help people make their voices known in the political world can be purchased for less than $100.

Personal Advocate generates letters and includes a data base of consumer groups and government agencies and officials. From Parsons Technology; phone 1-800-223-6925.

Write Your Congressman includes excellent up-to-date information on all 535 members of Congress. From Software International; phone 800-365-0606.

Federal SoapBox Software improves on both of the above and offers everything you will ever need to make your voice heard. The program is also updated, free-of-charge, every quarter. 1-800-989-7627.

Stewardship

1. Malcolm MacGregor, P.O. Box 82, Gresham, OR 97030. MacGregor is an excellent private consultant.

2. *"In Joy" Stewardship*, by John Maxwell, stresses tithing and is only for the strongest of churches, where accountability and discipleship are part of tradition. In Joy, Box 1700, Spring Valley, CA 92077

3. Nehemiah Ministries. Phone 612-435-2700.

4. Budgetshare, Box 460127, Houston, TX 77056. Phone 713-691-0849.

5. Discover the Joy is an excellent stewardship program from RSI, 12770 Merit Drive, Suite 900, Dallas, TX 75251. Phone 1-800-527-6824.

6. *The MISSING PIECE of Successful Living* contains an actual stewardship program used at Colonial Hills United Methodist Church during 1992. It includes a letter, articles for newsletters or bulletins, a calendar, and stewardship lessons for adult Sunday school classes. It is designed for mid- to large-sized churches. 54 pages. 21st Century Strategies, Inc., 1126 Whispering Sands, Port Aransas, TX 78373. Phone 512-749-5364; fax 512-749-5800. $20.00.

7. 21st Century Strategies, Inc. provides on-site services in conducting annual stewardship drives or capital fund drives for building purposes. 1126 Whispering Sands, Port Aransas, TX 78373. Phone 512-749-5364; fax 512-749-5800.

Sunday School

1. Kirchoff, Rich. *How to Start New Sunday School Classes*. 575 Lambuth Blvd., Jackson, TN 38301. Phone 901-427-8589.

2. Barger, Louise. *Growing Through the Sunday School*. P.O. Box 851, Valley Forge, PA 19482.

3. Berryman, Jerome. *Teaching Godly Play*. Nashville: Abingdon, 1995.

Teaching Churches

1. Teaching Church Network, P.O. Box 39282, Minneapolis, MN 55439-0208. Phone 612-942-9866; fax 612-949-6711. Participation in this organization is by invitation only, but you can approach them with your interest. If a church wishes to participate in this network, it cannot be conflicted and uncertain about its mission.

Telemarketing

1. "The Phone Is for You," can be ordered from Church Growth Development International, 420 W. Lambert Rd., Suite E, Brea, CA 92621. Phone 714-990-9551. For help designing the mail-outs, see Petrogram (item 3 under Direct Mail).

2. For a wide variety of excellent examples of telephone surveys, see George Barna, *Church Marketing* (Ventura, Calif.: Regal Books, 1992).

Women's Ministries

1. Schaller, Lyle E. *44 Ways to Revitalize the Women's Organization*. Nashville: Abingdon, 1990.

Worship

1. *Growth Plus Worship Attendance Crusade Guide*. Discipleship Resources, Box 189, Nashville, TN 37202. Phone 615-340-7285.

2. *Worship Leader* is an excellent monthly magazine for worship leaders. P.O. Box 40985, Nashville, TN 37204.

3. *House of Worship*, a newsletter, may be ordered by calling 1-800-245-7664. $29.95 per year.

4. Wilson, Carol. *The Church Concert Series Handbook*. Coral Ridge Presbyterian Church, 5555 N. Federal Highway, Fort Lauderdale, FL 33308. Phone 305-491-1104.

5. Dobson, Ed. *Starting A Seeker Sensitive Service*. Grand Rapids, Mich.: Zondervan, 1993. This is a very creative book.

6. Wright, Timothy. *A Community of Joy*. Nashville: Abingdon, 1994. This book provides help in developing a contemporary service.

7. The Sunday School Board of the Southern Baptist Convention has worship resources for the small church. Order a catalogue by calling 1-800-458-2772.

8. *Demonstrations of Contemporary Worship* is a ninety-minute video including the story of how First United Methodist Church of Jonesboro, Arkansas, began its blue-jeans worship service in their gym and a one-hour walk-through of how to plan a contemporary Saturday night or Sunday morning service. 21st Century Strategies, Inc., 1126 Whispering Sands, Port Aransas, TX 78373. Phone 512-749-5364; fax 512-749-5800. $39.95.

9. *Worship in the 1990s* includes samples of contemporary worship, confidential response cards for registering attendance, nursery tips, and many suggestions about worship for our time as well as suggestions about how to start a second service. 38 pages. 21st Century Strategies, Inc., 1126 Whispering Sands, Port Aransas, TX 78373. Phone 512-749-5364; fax 512-749-5800. $7.00.

Youth

1. Search Institute, 700 S. Third St., Minneapolis, MN 55415. Phone 1-800-888-7828. Write for their catalogue. Their quarterly newsletter, *Source*, is worth ordering.

2. *Healthy Communities, Healthy Youth*. Search Institute, 700 S. Third St., Minneapolis, MN 55415. Phone 1-800-888-7828. $10.00 plus $1.50 for shipping and handling.

3. Benson, Peter L. *The Troubled Journey: Full Report*. Search Institute, 700 S. Third St., Minneapolis, MN 55415. Phone 1-800-888-7828. Surveys 47,000 sixth- through twelfth-graders and suggests strategies for those who work with youth.

4. Andress, Shelby. *Working Together with Youth*. Search Institute, 700 S. Third St., Minneapolis, MN 55415. Phone 1-800-888-7828. A practical approach with specific instruments to help youth workers identify and implement programs.

5. Sun Cities Ministries, Willow Creek Community Church, P.O. Box 3168, South Barrington, IL 60011-3188.

6. *Youth Leaders Update* is an audio cassette series that provides nine tapes per year with listening guides. $72.00 for the first year. Fuller Institute, Box 919901, Pasadena, CA 91109. Phone 1-800-999-9578. These may or may not be available in the future, but the back copies are great.

RECOMMENDED READING

The following are some of the best books available today on all aspects of ministry. Many of theses books are also listed in the Recommended Resources section under the various areas of ministry to which they relate. All of these books are outstanding, but I have marked books of exceptional value and interest with up to four stars.

Bardwick, Judith. *Danger in the Comfort Zone*. New York: American Management Association, 1991. ★★★★
Barker, Joel. *Future Edge or Paradigms*. New York: Morrow, 1992. ★★★★
Barna, George. *Church Marketing*. Ventura, Calif.: Regal Books, 1992. ★★★
———. *The Invisible Generation*. Glendale, Calif.: Barna Research Group, 1992.
———. *Turnaround Churches*. Ventura, Calif.: Regal Books, 1993. ★★★★
———. *User Friendly Churches*. Ventura, Calif.: Regal Books, 1991.
Benveniste, Guy. *The Twenty-First Century Organization*. San Francisco: Jossey-Bass, 1994. ★★★★
Bergquist, William. *The Post Modern Organization*. San Francisco: Jossey-Bass, 1993. ★★★★
Block, Peter. *Stewardship*. San Francisco: Berrett Koehler, 1993.
Boutilier, Robert. *Targeting Families*. New York: American Demographics, 1992.
Bridges, William. *Job Shift*. New York: Addison Wesley, 1994.
Brueggemann, Walter. *Biblical Perspective on Evangelism*. Nashville: Abingdon, 1993. ★★★

Callahan, Kennon. *Effective Church Leadership*. San Francisco: HarperSanFrancisco, 1990. ★★★★
———. *Giving and Stewardship in an Effective Church*. San Francisco: HarperSanFrancisco, 1992.
———. *Twelve Keys to an Effective Church*. San Francisco: HarperSanFrancisco, 1983.
Chandler, Russell. *Racing Toward 2001*. Grand Rapids, Mich.: Zondervan, 1992. ★★★★
Coupland, Douglas. *Life After God*. New York: Pocket Books, 1994. ★★★
Crandall, Ron. *Turnaround Strategies for the Small Church*. Nashville: Abingdon, 1995.

Davis, Stanley. *Future Perfect*. New York: Addison Wesley, 1987. ★★★★
Dobson, Ed. *Starting a Seeker Sensitive Service*. Grand Rapids, Mich.: Zondervan, 1993. ★★★★
Drucker, Peter. *The Effective Executive*. New York: Harper Business, 1993. ★★★★
———. *Managing the Non-Profit Organization*. New York: Harper Collins, 1990.
———. *The Post-Capitalist Society*. New York: Harper Business, 1993. ★★★★
Dunn, William. *The Baby Bust*. New York: American Demographics, 1993. ★★

Easum, William M. *The Church Growth Handbook*. Nashville: Abingdon, 1990.
——. *Dancing with Dinosaurs*. Nashville: Abingdon, 1993. ★★★★
——. *How to Reach Baby Boomers*. Nashville: Abingdon, 1991. ★★
——. *Sacred Cows Make Gourmet Burgers*. Nashville: Abingdon, 1995. ★★★★

Friedman, Edwin. *Friedman's Fables*. New York: Guilford, 1990. ★★★★
——. *Generation to Generation*. New York: Guilford, 1985.

Galloway, Dale. *20/20 Vision*. Portland: Scott Publishing, 1986. ★★★
George, Carl. *Prepare Your Church for the Future*. New York: Revel, 1992. ★★★
Gerber, Michael. *The E Myth*. New York: Harper Business, 1986.

Hamal, Gary, and C. K. Prahalad. *Competing for the Future*. Boston: Harvard Business School, 1994.
Haugk, Kenneth. *Antagonists in the Church*. Minneapolis: Augsburg, 1988.
Hunter, George S. III. *Church for the Unchurched*. Nashville: Abingdon, 1996.
——. *How to Reach Secular People*. Nashville: Abingdon, 1992. ★★★

Imparato, Nicholas. *Jumping the Curve*. San Francisco: Jossey-Bass, 1994.

Joiner, Donald W., and Norma Wimberly. *The Abingdon Guide to Funding Ministry*, vol. 1. Abingdon, 1995.

Kami, Michael. *Trigger Points*. New York: McGraw-Hill, 1988.
Keck, Leander. *The Church Confident*. Nashville: Abingdon, 1993. ★★★
Korten, David. *When Corporations Ruled the World*. San Francisco: Berrett-Koehler, 1995.

Laboron, Graham. *The Horizontal Revolution*. San Francisco: Jossey-Bass, 1994. ★★
Leas, Speed. *Moving Your Church Through Conflict*. Washington. D.C.: Alban Institute, 1985.
Lucas, *The T-Form Organization*. San Francisco: Jossey-Bass, 1996.

Mahedy, William, and Janet Bernardi. *A Generation Alone*. Downers Grove, Ill.: InterVarsity Press, 1994.
Malphurs, Aubrey. *Pouring New Wine into New Wine Skins*. Grand Rapids, Mich.: Baker Books, 1993.
Mead, Loren. *The Once and Future Church*. Washington, D.C.: Alban Institute, 1991. ★★★★
Menking, Stanley, and Barbara Wendland. *God's Partners*. Valley Forge: Judson, 1993. ★
Miller, Herb. *Connecting with God*. Nashville: Abingdon, 1994. ★★
——. *How to Develop a Vital Congregation*. Nashville: Abingdon, 1990.
Mintzberg, Henry. *The Rise and Fall of Strategic Planning*. New York: Free Press, 1994.
Mitchelle, Susan. *The Official Guide to the Generations*. New York: American Demographics, 1995.
Morton, Nelle. *The Journey Home*. Boston: Beacon, 1985.
Murren, Doug. *The Baby Boomerang*. Ventura, Calif.: Regal Books, 1990.

Naisbitt, John, and Patricia Aburdene. *Megatrends 2000*. New York: Morrow, 1990. ★★★★
Neighbor, Ralph. *Where Do We Go from Here*. Houston: Touch, 1990. ★★★

Peck, Scott. *A World Waiting to Be Born*. New York: Bantam, 1993. ★★
Peters, Tom. *Thriving on Chaos*. New York: Harper, 1987.
Pinchot, G. & E. *The End of Bureaucracy and the Rise of the Intelligent Organization*. San Francisco: Berrett-Koehler, 1993. ★★★★

Redfield, James. *The Celestine Prophecy*. New York: Warner Books, 1993. ★★★★
Roozen, David, and C. Kirk Hadaway. *Church and Denominational Growth*. Nashville: Abingdon, 1993. ★★★★

Roxburg, Alan. *Reaching a New Generation*. Downers Grove, Ill.: InterVarsity, 1993. ★★★★
Russel, Cheryl. *One Hundred Predictions for the Baby Boom*. New York: Plenum, 1987. ★★

Sample, Tex. *Hard Living People and Mainstream Christians*. Nashville: Abingdon, 1993.
———. *U.S. Lifestyles and Mainline Churches*. Louisville: Westminster, 1990. ★★★
Savage, John. *The Bored and Apathetic Church Member*. Reynoldsburg, Oh.: L.E.A.D. Publishers/John Savage, 1979.
Schaller, Lyle E. *Building Bridges to the Twenty-First Century*. Nashville: Abingdon, 1994.
———. *Center City Churches*. Nashville: Abingdon, 1993.
———. *The Change Agent*. Nashville: Abingdon, 1972.
———. *44 Ways to Expand the Financial Base of Your Church*. Nashville: Abingdon, 1989.
———. *44 Ways to Revitalize the Women's Organization*. Nashville: Abingdon, 1990.
———. *The Multiple Staff and the Larger Church*. Nashville: Abingdon, 1980. ★★★★
———. *The Seven-Day-A-Week Church*. Nashville: Abingdon, 1992. ★★★★
Schwartz, Peter. *The Art of the Long View*. New York: Doubleday, 1991.
Senge, Peter. *The Fifth Discipline*. New York: Doubleday, 1990.
Shawchuck, Norman, and Gustave Rath. *Benchmarks of Quality in the Church*. Nashville: Abingdon, 1994.
Shawchuck, Norman, et al. *Marketing for Congregations*. Nashville: Abingdon, 1992. ★★★★
Slaughter, Michael. *Spiritual Entrepreneurs*. Nashville: Abingdon, 1995. ★★
Strauss, William, and Neil Howe. *Generations*. New York: Morrow, 1992. ★★★★
Strobel, Lee. *Inside the Mind of Unchurched Harry and Mary*. Grand Rapids, Mich.: Zondervan, 1993. ★★★★
Sweet, Leonard. *Faithquakes*. Nashville: Abingdon, 1994. ★★★★
———. *Quantum Spirituality*. Dayton: Whale, 1991. ★★★★

Tipler, Frank. *The Physics of Immortality*. New York: Doubleday, 1994. ★★★★
Toffler, Alvin. *Powershift*. New York: Bantam, 1990. ★★★★
Turner, Charles. *Creating Corporate Culture*. New York: Addison Wesley, 1990.

Warren, Rick. *The Purpose of Driven Church*. Grand Rapids, Mich.: Zondervan, 1995.
Waldrop, Mitchell. *Complexity*. New York: Simon and Schuster, 1992. ★★
Walton, Mary. *The Deming Management Method*. New York: Perigee, 1986.
Wellins, Richard S., et al. *Empowered Teams*. San Francisco: Jossey-Bass, 1991.
Wheatly, Margaret. *Leadership and the New Science*. San Francisco: Berrett-Koehler, 1992. ★★★
Wright, Timothy. *The Community of Joy*. Nashville: Abingdon, 1994. ★★★★

Appendixes

1. EVALUATING THE CHURCH BULLETIN AND NEWSLETTER

The Bulletin

1. Does your bulletin include a regular place (not on an insert) that welcomes the visitors and tells them how to
   a. get information about Christianity;
   b. get information about Jesus Christ;
   c. find out how to join the church (this is not as important as items a and b)?

2. Is your bulletin easy to read with lots of white space?

3. Does your bulletin have an abundance of words or phrases that the unchurched might not know?

4. Is your bulletin designed more for a person who has never attended your church than for the members?

5. You can improve your bulletin using the following tips:
   a. Keep it simple and avoid clutter.
   b. Limit yourself to two fonts—one for headlines and one for the body. Avoid fonts that are hard to read, even if you like the way they look.
   c. Avoid using all capital letters. Using all capital letters to emphasize a point is like yelling. No one likes to be yelled at.
   d. Drastically limit the use of clip art and fancy borders.
   e. Keep column widths between two and four inches. Anything narrower or wider is difficult to read.
   f. Keep regular sections in the same places—especially the section that welcomes guests. Don't make readers hunt for what they need.
   g. Keep a file of well-designed bulletins to stimulate your ideas.

The Newsletter

1. Is it mailed at least monthly to everyone, including first-time visitors?

2. Can it be read in five minutes?

3. Is it free of poems or cute sayings?

2. EVALUATING THE SITE, PROPERTY, AND FACILITIES

Accessibility

1. Does the church have any signs at various intersections pointing the way to the church? What do these signs tell you about the church? Are they neat and freshly painted? Are they obscured by brush or trees?

2. How easy is it to find the nursery, sanctuary, and the pastor's office without having to ask for directions?

3. Important property considerations:
   a. On how many acres does the church sit? How much of the land is usable? If your goal is to become a regional church, you need a minimum of eight acres, but thirty or more is better.
   b. How many sets of stairs does your church have? We are in a one-story world. The more stairs you have, the fewer people you will have at church in the twenty-first century. The country is getting older.
   c. How bright is the sanctuary? Bright is better than dim. It is hard to celebrate in a dark room.
   d. Is the location of the church visible to those passing by on major traffic arteries? Most churches are located five hundred feet off the beaten path.
   e. How wide are the halls? The minimum acceptable width is ten feet.

The Nursery

1. What is the appearance of the nursery? (How neat is it? Are things stored in the nursery that have nothing to do with infants? Is the carpet clean? Are the walls freshly painted? Are there windows?)

2. Is the nursery on the same floor as the sanctuary?

3. Is there a sign at every turn of the corridor showing the direction to the nursery and to the sanctuary?

4. Every room should have at least one paid worker. This person should be able to work with volunteers. This person should be regular in attendance so that the children see a familiar face when they arrive. You will have to pay this person well in order to ensure consistency.

150

5. Larger churches should employ a part-time person who oversees all of the nurseries, hires paid help, and recruits volunteers.

6. Require people to sign in when they leave children, even if the people are members of the church. It is best if you require them to leave their drivers' licenses when they leave their children. Do not allow a spouse to pick up the child; in today's world, it is impossible to know from week to week who is separated or divorced, and churches are becoming easy places in which to carry out noncustodial kidnapping.

7. Place a name tag on each child as he or she enters the room.

8. Give parents a pager or beeper that vibrates so that you can summon them if there is a problem. These instruments are not expensive anymore.

9. Give all first-time parents a brochure telling them about the nursery. Include such details as the procedures regarding dropping off and picking up children, how often you change the sheets and clean the toys, and so forth.

10. Give your nursery workers regular training.

11. Anytime the carpet has a stain that cannot be cleaned, replace the carpet, even if it is rather new.

12. Sanitize the room and the toys after each use.

13. Keep the nurseries free of hazards. Do not allow parents to bring anything hot, such as coffee or tea, into the rooms. Do not stack things that toddlers could pull off on top of cabinets. Provide storage cabinets high enough that children cannot reach them. Most cleaning supplies should never be left in any nursery area.

14. Redecorate the entire nursery complex each year. Repaint and remove any damaged equipment, toys, or carpet.

15. Do not use the nursery for storage of any kind.

16. Use the nursery as an opportunity for evangelism:
    a. Take a picture of each first-time child and place it on the bulletin board. If the child does not return within three weeks, send the picture to the parents telling them you are still holding a place for their child.
    b. Send a letter of congratulation to the parents of all newborn children. If you have a large number of older adults, you may consider starting a "surrogate grandparent" ministry. Let new parents know about this ministry, in case they need help rearing their child.
    c. Many churches ask new parents (members of their church) if they would like to have a lawn sign for a month that reads, "Newest member of (name of church)." The signs are either blue or pink and have a picture of stork carrying a baby.

Construction Issues

For churches that are planning to build, the following is a suggested chronology to follow as you move into your building program.

1. Consultant planning.

2. Decision to move forward.

3. Building and program committee selection.

4. Selection and approval of architect.

5. Preliminary drawings.

6. Completed drawings.

During these preliminary stages, keep in mind the following ten steps toward improving your church's appearance:

a. Improve your curb appeal. The property needs to say "Welcome" to people passing by. It helps to create a point of interest that draws people's attention.

b. Create well-planned entrances to the property. Entrances should not be bottlenecks and should facilitate a safe and natural flow. They should not be more than six hundred feet from the parking lot.

c. Signs should be legible and perpendicular to the street. Drive by your church and clock the interval between when you can first read the sign and the time you pass it. The entire sign should be easily readable in that time period.

d. Develop a landscaped parking lot that provides one space for every two people at the time when the most people are on the property. Reserve spaces for guests.

e. Provide security so that people will feel safe. Create an open feeling with no oversized bushes or hiding places. Good lighting is essential in the parking lot, entry way, and hallways.

f. Develop the site so that activity is clearly visible from the street. Playgrounds, parking lots, and major entrances should be visible to those passing by.

g. Maintain the facilities and grounds. Always keep the lawn mowed.

h. Concentrate on visitor-friendly touches, such as parking lot greeters and valets to assist elderly people and single parents with parking. Make sure welcome centers are highly visible.

i. Make sure the entrance to the sanctuary is large enough and has enough doors (usually two doors for every hundred people in worship). It is best if the lobby exits to the outside (rather than to an inside hallway, for example).

7. Building fund campaign.

8. Building fund celebration.

9. Completed bids.

10. Authorization of construction.

11. Ground breaking.

12. As you begin building, post a sign on the site telling the community what you are doing and when you plan to be finished.

13. Community outreach. When the facilities are completed have an opening celebration, and invite the community to attend. Send out invitations to all the families and individuals in the area asking them to join you for this great moment in the life of your church. Plan a way that those who do show up are encouraged to give you their names, addresses and phone numbers, and then follow up on them. You will not have a high number of visitors, but the ones who do show up will be excellent potential new members or converts.

14. First Sunday celebration. Ask the Mayor (or another city official) to attend the celebration and take a small part.

15. Celebration year. Use the entire following year to celebrate this momentous event in the life of your church.

For churches that are thinking about building, the following questions and suggestions are intended to help you determine whether you need or are ready for a new facility.

1. What ministries will occur in this facility?

2. Will the people walk or drive to this facility?
3. What are the accessibility needs of this facility?
   a. What is the average age of the person using the facility now and forty years from now?
   b. Will we include ministries for those with mobility and hearing difficulties?

4. Will the number of people using this facility fluctuate throughout the year?

5. Is the entrance to the present facility large enough to encourage people to enter and to fellowship?

6. Do the hallways in the present facility encourage conversation?

7. Is the nursery accessible?
   a. It should be on the same level as the sanctuary and as close to the sanctuary as possible.
   b. Is the area safe from someone entering from an outside door?
   c. Is there a dutch door separating the parents from the children?
   d. Is there separate space for "cribbers," "crawlers," and "walkers"?
   e. Are there thirty square feet per child in each of the areas?
   f. Is there a sink and changing table in each room?
   g. Can the nursery be restricted to nursery use only?

8. The following questions apply to the sanctuary.
   a. Is the seating based on twenty-two to twenty-four inches per person?
   b. Is there a parking space for every two people?
   c. Can the entrance be seen from the street?
   d. Is the sanctuary set back from the street corner, and does the parking area wrap around the sanctuary? Is at least a portion of the parking area visible from the street and not entirely hidden by the sanctuary.
   e. If the sanctuary is used three or more times on Sunday morning, is the sanctuary's capacity twice as large as the educational facility's capacity?
   f. Can the sanctuary be used while Sunday school is taking place?
   g. Do the exits encourage everyone to exit into a large lobby that is also a fellowship area?
   h. Is there a place in the lobby for a book table or bookstore?
   i. Will the sanctuary be designed primarily for preaching or for the administration of the sacraments?
   j. Has the use of visual media been taken into consideration?
   k. Is there a good sound system and are there enough electrical outlets?
   l. Is there room on stage for drama presentations and an orchestra?
   m. What role do we want the choir or choirs to play?
   n. What will this sanctuary look like when it is half full?
   o. Can additions be made to this sanctuary in the future without it looking as if it has been altered?
   p. Is there a registration area in the lobby?
   q. Have parking spaces for visitors been considered?
   r. Have parking spaces for single parents been considered?
   s. Will the people we are targeting prefer pews or padded theater seats?
   t. Are the pews too long?

u. Is there an entrance to the sanctuary within six hundred feet of the most distant space in the parking lot?

v. Is the pastor's office accessible from both the inside and the outside of the building?

9. The following questions apply to educational facilities.
   a. Is everyone aware that educational facilities never pay for themselves?
   b. Have we considered two sessions of Sunday school or alternate sites for classes or small groups augmenting Sunday school?
   c. Are the classrooms designed to be attractive meeting rooms first and classrooms second?
   d. Is each room going to be without sound overflow from other rooms?
   e. Have we taken into account that multimedia presentations will be essential in the twenty-first century?
   f. Will the first unit include one large room that can be used as a large lecture class led by the pastor?
   g. Is the lighting bright and cheerful?
   h. Do the classrooms vary in size?

10. The following questions apply to the office area.
    a. Is the office a self-contained unit in terms of heating, cooling, security, and restrooms?
    b. Is the staff space designed for growth?
    c. Does the staff space have its own private conference room?
    d. Is the area designed for computer networking?
    e. Is there a large space where office volunteers can work during the week?
    f. Have you spent disproportionately more on the office area than on the nursery, parking lot , or parlor?
    g. Has some member who is knowledgeable about business environments looked over the plans for the office?
    h. Has "flow" (the office traffic pattern) been considered?

11. What will be the first impression on the people passing by?
    a. Is the primary sign readable to people who pass by?
    b. Have we considered using flower beds for color?
    c. Does a person standing in the parking lot know where to go to find the sanctuary or a place for information?

12. Have we considered the appropriate number of restrooms, and do they include changing areas for infants?

13. Is there a room for choir rehearsal where the choir cannot be heard in the sanctuary?

14. Have energy costs been considered?

15. Have we installed air-conditioning so that we can be a twelve-month church?

For congregations who are ready to select a new site for a church, asking the following questions about the sites you are considering should help you make the right choice.

1. Is there drainage and storm water control?

2. What are the subsoil conditions?

3. Is there access to public utilities?

4. Are we considering enough acres?

5. Are their any government restrictions against churches building on this property?

6. Is this property accessible?

7. Is this property highly visible?

8. What are the future plans of the city for the streets in this area?

For churches who are ready to choose an architect, the following questions are intended to help you evaluate your candidates.

1. Does this person exhibit creativity in design and process?

2. How flexible is this person? Will he or she work with us to build what we want, or will he or she build what he or she wants?

3. Would this be someone we would want to work with in the future?

4. What is the integrity of this person's earlier projects—both structurally and functionally?

5. How accurate have this person's estimates been on recent projects?

6. Does this person have access to computer software that will allow you to see three dimensional pictures of his or her designs?

7. How good is this person in executing his or her designs?

8. Is this person capable of meeting your deadlines?

9. Will this person be the principal person working on your project, or will a junior person be responsible?

10. Is this person able to work with other consultants or is he or she a loner?

11. Does this person have access to other good, sound architects or consultants?

12. Are this person and the person from the church assigned to supervise this project compatible?

13. What is this person's fee structure?

3. How to Use the Bonus Spreadsheet Disk

The following information will help you make the most of the bonus spreadsheets on the floppy disk that comes with *The Complete Ministry Audit*.

Introduction

You might prefer to print this text file (ASCII) from your word processor for easier reference as you complete the audit.

As a convenience, the spreadsheet disk contains two sets of files that can improve your methods for collecting the data required for group or personal study of *The Complete Ministry Audit*. Lotus 2.3 files are DOS files and can be transferred to most Windows spreadsheet programs. Excel 5.0 files are portable to most Windows-based spreadsheet programs. Before inputting data in any of the files, it would be prudent to make a backup copy of the disk. You can then use the files again at a later date or restore a file that you want to do over.

These files are offered as a bonus to *The Complete Ministry Audit*. Therefore, please secure the help of a person in your congregation who has a basic understanding of spreadsheet math. With the exception of the STAFF1.* worksheet, all the worksheets use only one formula: averaging. The formula for averaging will be added by you after all the data has been collected. The spreadsheets are not complicated, but NO TECHNICAL OR TRAINING SUPPORT in the use of the ministry audit or in the formation of spreadsheets is offered or implied by the publisher or the author of the workbook.

When your audit is complete, the author is willing to analyze your audit (for a fee). You may contact him at 512-749-5364.

Instructions for Using the Excel Worksheets

The following worksheets are included on your bonus spreadsheet disk in the directory labelled EXCEL.

BODY1.XLS
BODY1ENT.XLS
BODY2.XLS

BODY2ENT.XLS
BODY3.XLS
BODY3ENT.XLS

STAFF1.XLS
STFF1ENT.XLS
STAFF2.XLS
STFF2ENT.XLS
STAFF3.XLS
STFF3ENT.XLS

WORSHIP.XLS
WRSHPENT.XLS

The worksheets with "ENT.XLS" in the filename are data entry worksheets.

The worksheets without "ENT" in the filename are survey sheets that are provided for your convenience. You may print and copy any of these worksheets at your discretion. They have become your property.

Before you begin work on the Excel sheets, please make a backup copy of the diskette on another floppy disk or in a separate directory on your hard drive. If you need help with copying files or disks, see your computer manuals or help system.

Instructions for distributing and compiling the survey sheets are in the book. Follow the audit as outlined in the book and use the surveys in the audit. You may print as many copies of the surveys as you need to distribute within your church.

When learning how to construct simple spreadsheets, please use the help menu in Excel. When you are ready to tally up the results of the surveys, you will use the "*ENT.XLS" sheets. For example, to tally the results of the Official Body Worksheet (BODY1.XLS), you will use the corresponding data entry worksheet (BODY1ENT.XLS).

Open the worksheet that corresponds to the survey you wish to tally. The first empty column is column B. You will leave this column to hold the averages, which will be explained later.

Begin in column C, on the row "NAMES." Key in the name of the person who filled out the survey you wish to enter. Or, if you are using anonymous numbered surveys, key in the survey number.

Press [Enter].

Move down column C until you are in the cell on the row "Q1."

Key in the survey answer for question 1. This question should be answered with a number from 1 to 10. Key this number into the cell and press [Enter]. If the respondent did not answer this question, leave the cell blank. Do not enter a zero (0).

Continue moving down column C, keying in the quantitative responses for this survey. A list of nonquantitative questions appears at the bottom of the column. The text of the questions for this worksheet are at the bottom of the sheet, for easy reference or study.

When you have completed filling in all the responses for this survey, press [Ctrl-Home] to return to the top of the page.

Move to the cell in column D, on the row "NAMES." Continue to fill in the surveys as outlined above for each person who completed a particular form.

When all the surveys have been entered on a particular sheet, you will insert the AVERAGE formula to ascertain the average response for each question.

Move to column B, which you left blank. You will insert the formula for averages in column B.

Move down column B to the row "Q1."

From the main menu, select Insert/Function . . . .

Select Function/Category/Statistical from the list of function categories in the left window. If you do not have a category Statistical, select category All.

Select Function/Name/Average from the list of function names in the right window. Be sure that you have the correct function, as some function names are spelled nearly the same.

Click the Next> button at the bottom of the Insert/Function . . . dialogue box. In the arguments box, you may key in the cell addresses you wish to average (e.g., C12:G12), or you may mark the area on your worksheet at this time by selecting the cells with your mouse or keyboard. Select the cells only in the row (not the column) for the question you are averaging. You will only average one row at a time.

Click the Finish> button at the bottom of the Insert/Function . . . dialogue box.

Excel will insert the average result for that row. Then copy this formula down column B, where an average for each row is desired. Consult the Excel help system if you do not know how to copy cells.

Excel will shift the average down the rows to correspond to the responses keyed in for each question and refigure the average based on those numbers.

All the worksheets use the same procedure—averaging—except for STFF1ENT.XLS.

Comments on STFF1ENT.XLS

Most of the questions on the Staff 1 worksheet are nonquantitative. For advanced users of spreadsheets, the quantitative audit questions have been isolated, and a few basic formulas have been protected in the file STFF1ENT.XLS. Load the file into Excel and use these tables and percentages to gather data about your church. Again, no technical support is implied or provided by the publisher, yet this spreadsheet can save the knowledgeable computer user several hours of setting up formulas or rerecording data.

Instructions for Using Lotus Files

The following Lotus 2.3 files are available on the spreadsheet disk under the directory a:\LOTUS123\:

BODY1.WK1
BODY1ENT.WK1
BODY2.WK1

BODY2ENT.WK1
BODY3.WK1
BODY3ENT.WK1

STAFF1.WK1
STFF1ENT.WK1
STAFF2.WK1
STFF2ENT.WK1
STAFF3.WK1
STFF3ENT.WK1

WORSHIP.WK1
WRSHPENT.WK1

The worksheets with "ENT.WK1" in the filename are data entry worksheets. The worksheets without "ENT" in the filename are survey sheets. You may print and copy any of these worksheets at your discretion. They have become your property.

Before you begin work on the Lotus sheets, please make a backup copy of the diskette on another disk or in a separate directory on your hard drive. If you need help with copying files, see your computer manual or help system.

Instructions for distributing and compiling the survey sheets are in the book. Follow the audit as outlined in the book and use the surveys in the audit. You may print as many copies of the surveys as you need to distribute within your church.

When learning how to construct simple spreadsheets, please use the help menu in Lotus. When you are ready to tally up the results of the surveys, you will use the "*ENT.WK1" sheets. For example, to tally the results of the Official Body Worksheet (BODY1.WK1), you will use the corresponding data entry worksheet (BODY1ENT.WK1).

Open the worksheet that corresponds to the survey you wish to tally. The first empty column is column B. You will leave this column to hold the averages, which will be explained later.

Begin in column C, on the row "NAMES." Key in the name of the person who filled out the survey you wish to enter. Or, if you are using anonymous numbered surveys, key in the survey number.

Press [Enter].

Move down column C until you are in the cell on the row "Q1."

Key in the survey answer for question 1. This question should be answered with a number from 1 to 10. Key this number into the cell and press [Enter]. If the respondent did not answer this question, leave the cell blank. Do not enter a zero (0).

Continue moving down column C, keying in the quantitative responses for this survey. A list of nonquantitative questions appears at the bottom of the column. The text of the questions for this worksheet are at the bottom of the sheet, for easy reference or study.

When you have completed filling in all the responses for this survey, press [Ctrl-Home] to return to the top of the page.

Move to the cell in column D, on the row "NAMES." Continue to fill in the surveys as outlined above for each person who completed a particular form.

When all the surveys have been entered on a particular sheet, you will insert the AVERAGE formula to ascertain the average response for each question. Make a note of the final column that contains data. Let's say, for example, that the final column is J.

Move to column B, which you left blank . You will insert the formula for averages in column B. Move down column B to the row "Q1" (containing question 1).

Type the following formula, for example, into the cell: @AVG(C12.J12). The average response for question 1 will appear when you press [Enter]. You are now ready to copy this formula down column B to each row where an average is desired. Consult your Lotus help system if you do not know how to copy cells.

Comments on STFF1ENT.WK1

Most of the questions on the Staff 1 worksheet are nonquantitative. For advanced users of spreadsheets, the quantitative audit questions have been isolated, and a few basic formulas have been protected in the file STFF1ENT.WK1. Load the file into Lotus and use these tables and percentages to gather data about your church. Again, no technical support is implied or provided by the publisher, yet this spreadsheet can save the knowledgeable computer user several hours of setting up formulas or rerecording data.